An Immigrant's Tale
From Freedom to Slavery in the 21st Century

To: Aide
Thank you for your support!

Debbie
March '23

Cover design and illustration by Robert Wallman

Available at:
www.deborahepeters.com
and
www.amazon.com

Preface

I left my sweet smelling land of mangoes and guava,
To come to this place,
A noxious city of rotted foods in the summer and all time
pollution,
To learn that there's racism and discrimination, jealousy and
hatred,
Ultimate envy of everyone and allegiance to no one and
nothing.
These are things I learned here in America.

I learned to disrespect my fellow man,
Spit where he walks and despise him for his lack of culture
Hate him for his hatred of others
Love him because there's no one else to love and
Have children where there's no hope for a rewarding future.

Did I make a mistake? I would say I did.
I can close my eyes and remember the beautiful sunny days,
cool breezes blowing through my hair,
Fresh air, good food, happy people, loving and loyal families
and then reopen them to the reality of the dark and callous
land I now reside.

Oh beautiful America what lies you preach,
There's no freedom of speech and
No liberty and justice for all,
Such is for only for those that can afford to pay for it and not
for me.

By: Me

This book is dedicated to my children
For all that you have suffered and enjoyed
I only wanted the best for you

Thanks to all whose stories have helped make this compilation a piece well worth reading

CHAPTER ONE

Well, it's November, 2009, 22 years and 4 months since I first arrived at John F. Kennedy International airport in New York City. I finally have it; the proverbial 'Green Card'. So freaking what? Really, what does it do for me now? The economy is in the tank; there are no jobs and I am forced to do temporary work assignments for money that doesn't even allow me to pay rent if I had to. I'm an Executive Assistant/Office Manager and work in corporate America. I've singlehandedly sacrificed and taken care of myself and my kids (Adam 23, Danni 21 and Raven 11 - in that order) for the past 10 years and I find myself again at the mercy of a man. How and why did this happen? I can't even afford a trip to Florida much less outside the country......so what the heck good is this 'Green card' thing, really? I can't believe it. After all this time, life has come full circle for me and it's no fun at all!

I sit here deep in thought on the sofa. The aroma of Dettol and Murphy's Oil Soap emanating from the hard wood floors fill my nostrils and the cold, brisk winter air gently kisses my toes as it glides up the staircase from the front door. It's extremely cold this fall. After years of hardship and suffering at the hands of a man and men, I truly hope this one, sitting here totally focused on whatever he was doing on his computer is my 'bus stop' as he has always said since we first met. A man I allowed myself to love wholeheartedly and who I felt was 'the one'. No, not like Neo, but the one for me.

Jeopardy is on and Alex Tribeck is gaffing on the red headed chick who can't pronounce "salamander'. She has some kind of twisted tongue and keeps saying what sounds to me like "amalanther". Red heads are a little kooky I think. I slowly glance around at the 32 inch flat screen TV hung on the wall, contemporary beige and brown leather living room set, light brown panel wood, custom made blinds, does it make me happy – no. Was neither a superficial nor materialistic girl.

My father, for all his 'pointed out' flaws, didn't raise me that way. He himself was a country boy who fell for the city girl. My parents' opposing upbringing obstructed all they could teach my brothers and me of how to evaluate ourselves as individuals as well as others. My two younger brothers and I give everyone the benefit of the doubt, even the vagrant on the street, and will even venture so far as to marry and bear children for them too! That's what I did. You might say I'm just a stupid ass but only those raised in that environment can understand what I mean. The three of us made very similar mistakes and it all pertains to that simple but very important fact that we simply were not taught some of life's hard lessons. Such lessons can make or break a human being. But that's the past and this is now.

"We gonna eat or what?" His deep, baritone voice jolted me out of my pondering state. "Oh…." I immediately glanced at the cable box and noted the time. I jumped up to start dinner. It was already 7:30pm. He was sitting at his desk all the time I stared at that goofy red head on the television daydreaming. "Whachu wanna eat?" "Food," he said without once glancing away from his computer, all 160lbs of him in his 5'7" dark skinned, muscular and perfectly defined frame, busily shaking his left leg as he usually does when he's working on his contracts.

I've got the perfect man. He has his own business, a home office, makes good money and spends as much time with me as I want. It's overwhelming at times the tumultuous torrent of emotions that he stirs within me whilst the sight, scent and feel of him invades every cell in my body and every thought in my mind! The intensity of the passion between us is as potent as the day we met if not more so. It's been three years and together we have become a separate entity, an entirely different person, an entity that can be truly formidable to the layman dare he try to contest! Sometimes we are like two male lions fighting for leadership of the pride. Sometimes I let him win.

CHAPTER TWO

At the tender age of 20; I was already a wife and mother, customary of where I came from. We were bred to believe that you must get married and have children; it's what you are here on this Earth to do, as a woman. I followed the laws of my land perfectly. My mother was married and a mother of one at age 21 and so was I, right on target in her footsteps. Things were different in her day and time. She's gone now, to a higher and better plane.

I can recall that dreadful day. We caught an early movie, Will Smith's Wild, Wild West at the Linden Boulevard Multiplex in Brooklyn where we lived, me and the kids. We returned home around 5:30pm. It was August 15, 1999, a Sunday afternoon and a beautiful summer day in New York City. I was holding Raven, who was just 18 months at the time, as we entered the apartment and I saw the message light blinking on the answering machine. I went directly to it as if on auto pilot and pressed the play button. Raven was playing with a strand of my hair and just staring at my face with her big, dark eyes. She is a beautiful child. Light skinned with long, black curly hair and adorable pudgy cheeks to compliment her wide, bright eyes that could be compared to deep, dark pools in the moonlight. I heard a somewhat familiar voice coming from the machine, "Yeah Debbie, I'm calling to let you know that mummy passed away today ok? Alright." I stood motionless for what seemed like eons just staring at the machine, but it was certainly only seconds. I played the message again and still couldn't grasp the meaning of it. I know what it sounded like I heard but I couldn't quite understand the words nor recognize the voice. I came out of my stupor in a momentary flash; put the baby down to run around and decided to call my father to get to the bottom of this crazy message. My parents and youngest brother still lived in Trinidad. The voice could have been anyone of my male family members as they all have similar voices and the message was somewhat inaudible.

After what seemed like an eternity, someone picked up the phone at the other end, "Hello." It was my dad but he didn't sound quite like his usual self. The hair on the back of my neck rose, my stomach bottomed out and my extremities turned ice cold. Trying to sound calm I started, "Hello dad. Wah happun?" He said, "Your mummy passed away dis afternoon." The only other time I've ever heard my father sound so disheartened and seen him cry was back in 1973 when my youngest brother at that time, Cary, died just 2 weeks after he was born. He died of a malformed intestine doctors said. I asked again more urgently, "What happened?" He was obviously gathering his emotions to speak to me more freely. What is taking him so long?? I could hear Adam and Danni arguing in the back bedroom as usual and Raven was mulling around me like a busy bee whilst she half way watched cartoons on the television. Timmy Turner was making a wish in the distance. Boy did I wish I had some fairy god parents right now!

"Well", my dad began, "we went to church today and your mummy got vexed wit de priest. She didn' take her blood pressure medication today and she tole meh she was feelin' really nauseous when we got home. She started vomitin after a little while and den she started tellin meh her chest was hurting and she cyah breathe. Ah call yuh brodder quick and we help her get in de back seat of de car wit him while he hole her head up on his chest. We drove as fast as we could to Mount Hope Hospital. She died in the car. Brent was holdin her." I didn't say anything right away. "Are you okay?" I asked him. That might sound stupid but I couldn't think straight right then. "Is Brent okay? So what did they say she died of?" "Massive heart attack. Brent, I dunno how Brent doing nah but I ok." he said. Now the sounds around me became distorted and I felt like I might have been in a wind tunnel, alone and miserable just spinning around and around. I could barely see.

Mommy…..mommy…….MOMMY!!!!! I felt her pulling on my shirt hem and looked down at my baby as the sound of her voice slowly brought me out of that dark realm and back to reality. "One minute honey," I droned. "Mommy, can I have some juice?" I shouted to my older daughter, "Danni, give Raven some juice for me please!!!" I quickly returned to the conversation. My dad was quiet during this exchange. I could feel the heaviness of his mood through the phone across thousands of miles. It weighed heavily on my own heart. His silence was deafening. He suddenly said he needed to go since my mother's mother and brother had shown up at the house. "Ok. I will talk to you later den Dad. Love you." I hung up and looked around at the kids going through their regular routines and prayed that God would grant me life long enough to at least see them all reach a successful adult life.

Later on that night, while I lay in bed reminiscing of my childhood with my mother and feeling guilty about the poor relationship we had was when it hit me. I would not be able to go home for my own mother's funeral! Her first born and only daughter! I was still considered an "illegal alien" in the United States and if I left now, I would not be able to return for at least 10 years. This was the straw that broke the camel's back; the dam broke and the tears exploded from places that had remained dry for years. I could hear myself sobbing uncontrollably into my pillow in the still of the night and tried hard to muffle the sounds so as not to let the children hear and become upset, especially Raven who was fast asleep next to me. The realization was painfully harsh. I was enslaved by the land I occupied and unable to leave it. The strict immigration laws limit foreigners to animalistic and instinctive states of survival only.

CHAPTER THREE

Life began for me back in the beautiful Caribbean island of Trinidad in 1965, the land of paradise it's called. I enjoyed a good and privileged life there until I made the bold and probably the worst decision of my life to venture a life in the United States of America.

It's always sunny with brief periods of rain here and there. Unless it's the rainy season, like June thru October when it rains more than usual but there will still be many beautiful days to enjoy. The air smelled good after the rain. Clean and fresh.

We lived in a small urban city called Trincity. It was once the home to slave masters but was given out to privileged people who could afford them after the slave trade ended and the sugar factory was nationalized. The factory was just two streets from ours across the Beetham Highway (now the Churchill Roosevelt Hwy). It still functioned as a sugar production plant but with paid workers and not slaves. All the homes were built with a maid's quarters and were all ranch style, beautiful houses with front and back yards of plush lawns and mango, palm or banana trees. We had a Julie mango tree that was stunted. It never did grow past five foot. It was always a battle to see who would get to the ripened mangos first – us or any of our three German Shepherd dogs. The bedrooms' back doors opened to the back yard. The mango tree was directly outside of my bedroom and I would always peek at the mangoes as they blossomed so I could get to them first. The dogs usually beat me to the punch since their kennels were in the back yard and they roamed freely all day long. Once, I saw the dog going for a mango that I had my eye on for about a week and I flung open my back door screaming, "Aye! Leave dat mango boy!" His mouth was open and one tooth was ready to sink into the mango's skin when I grabbed and plucked it quickly from the tree. Snoopy looked at me with an expression that looked totally like, "WTF?" If only animals could talk I thought as I hurried back inside to enjoy my prize.

Our home had three bedrooms, two and a half baths, a TV room, a living and dining room, kitchen, maid's quarters that had its own bathroom and a den. All the bedrooms were at the back of the house. The main bathroom separated the two smaller bedrooms from the master bedroom. My brothers, Gordon and Brent shared a bedroom. We were quite comfortable. There was every convenience. Washer and dryer – even though we dried our clothes mostly on lines in the back using the glorious sunshine. The dryer was mainly for when it rained.

My dad had his own textiles import/export business and worked from a home office. My mom was a vice principal and secretary of a privately run Catholic High School which we all attended. My brothers and I all went to Catholic school our entire academic career.

In July of 1982, I graduated with seven O'levels and was the only student that year to receive an A in English throughout the entire school. I didn't really care about that. I never considered English a real subject. It was just common sense and so easy how could it be reasonably labeled a 'subject'? I was bumming about getting a C in Math and a B in Human Biology. Math I couldn't help, it was my Achilles heel, but I was supposed to get an A in HB. During my final exam I forgot the final stage of amino acid digestion and made up some crap that cost me the difference between an A and a B. I knew exactly what caused this result and was so angry with myself. I simply had a mental block that I couldn't bypass for anything during the exam.

I first met Wesley in August that same year and began working at the bank soon after we met. I was 17 at the time. My dad played tennis with the head of human resources of Republic Bank Limited (formerly Barclays Bank) and they arranged for me to take the entrance exam which I passed with a 99% score after finishing the test in just ten minutes. I noticed people murmuring around the office at my score. Apparently it was unusual that a girl this young had done better than most adults on the very same exam. I was a gifted student so my parents were not surprised at the result. Needless to say, I got the job as a clerk at Republic Bank.

I was a star in my branch and proud to be there. My dad took me to and from work daily, just as he did to and from school and anywhere else we had to go. No public transportation for us!

I never took a bus or taxi until I was almost 18! Sometimes Wesley would drop or pick me up from work if he had someone's car that he was fixing. He was an auto mechanic. A grease monkey as they're called. He didn't have his own car yet. He never did get a driver's license either come to think of it until we came to America.

I worked at the San Juan branch of Republic Bank on Second Avenue just off the Eastern Main road, one long block from the 'Quaysaay'. I wanted desperately to learn about life as other people had it. Thus began my fight for freedom from my parents' grip.

It all started when my co-workers began teasing me consistently about my dad bringing me to and taking me from work every day. They would say things the likes of, "de bat mobile outside boy", or, "yuh fadder watching yuh tru de glass gyrl, watch yuhself!" "Yuh chauffeur outside gyrl." I'd had it with the innuendos. I was going to find another way home if it killed me!

My friend and BFF till today, Sue, lived further east than me in a very remote area, up Lopinot Road. She is of Indian descent and had hair down to her butt. Hair that she wrapped and wrapped until it became a giant bun on the back of her tiny head. She's all of 5 ft. and weighed a whopping 90 lbs. I remember watching her perform this ritual with her hair every lunch time in the employee bathroom and one day I just couldn't hold it in any longer, "Why don't you just cut that ponytail off? Every day you do the same ting and have the same hairstyle. Why do you have all dat hair if all you do is tie it up? Get a nice hairstyle so you could look modern instead of like some beta." The next week she showed up with a sporty new hairdo that made her look totally different and quite chic. It was cool to see she took

15

my advice. Thankfully, I was no longer subjected to that daily scene in the bathroom. She also ran with my suggestion to change her name to Sue.

We first met when she joined the bank not long after me, and she introduced herself as Subaghwatee. I looked down into her eyes with raised eyebrows and a smirk on my face and said, "Well, if you doh mind, I goh call you Sue. I cyah see mehself saying that long name every time I have to call you. Ah might trip on meh tongue!" She laughed. She still uses that name today.

We soon became the best of friends. Sue had to travel the same route to get home as me so we became travel companions and she taught me how to take taxis and buses home. People called us Mutt and Jeff, comparing us to cartoon characters at the time – one being very tall and one very short. We didn't care. We enjoyed being together. After a few months passed Sue eventually bought her own car ending our rides home together. I really didn't want to travel home alone. Another colleague and friend, June began dropping me off home and sometimes, so did my boss, Mrs. Wong since they both went that way too. June and I were also gym buddies and went to the gym in El Dorado three times a week one day being Saturday. It was not far from home for either of us. She would come get me and we would go together. I was quite fortunate and felt grownup to be free of my suffocating parents.

Now, this job thing was only supposed to be for a little while until I go back to school to complete my A levels and then join the University. That obviously never happened. The salary I was making was good enough for me and I was tired of school. My starting salary at the bank was the same as my mother's then salary after her 21 years of service at the school. I also enjoyed the corporate environment. The bank also had a sports club for its employees which wasn't far from the branch so we would go hang out there many times and swim in the pool.

One Friday afternoon I found myself walking in the branch at the 3PM opening time with the customers, my bob length, dirty blond hair soaking wet and flat to my scalp, makeup all washed off and uniform stuck to my wet body. My friend Visham, forgot to pick me up from the sports club where I went swimming during the lunch recess. On Fridays, we had a wonderful 3 hour lunch break because the branch opened until 5 on that day. I too had lost track of the time and only realized the time after Visham arrived for me, which explains why I was still wet. Fortunately, we were able to get back to work just in time for the afternoon shift.

My boss, Mrs. Wong, just looked up at me over her glasses rim, shook her head at the sight of me and then looked back down at whatever papers she was reading on her desk. I went right to work and eventually dried off. I was not a vain girl and so didn't care what I might have looked like to the customers. As long as my job was done we were all squared. Of course I knew I was in for a good tongue lashing from Mrs. Wong but that was the worst she ever did. She went on and on during the ride home but I just let her go on and agreed with her all the way.

She was my surrogate mom and I had total respect for her. Not to mention she had a totally gorgeous son who had the hots for me after we made out one night at the nightclub in Valsayn, but we won't elaborate on that here. I was a star employee and a girl as far as it was, so I was always able to get away with 'murder' like they say. Life was good.

CHAPTER FOUR

Since I was the baby of the branch, I was always assigned a driver to chauffer me to and from every party that the branch had. They were always organizing one get together or another. They even helped me gain access to night clubs since I was underage. They were just awesome people and we had lots of fun together in and out of work.

When I turned 19, I bought my own car. A Mazda 323, a small and convenient car. It was tan and the license plates read PAS 9984. The plates of today are well past that series I know. At 19 I had already known and was dating Wesley for two years. My parents did everything in their power to end the relationship but to no avail. He had some qualities I admired. Even though he came from a less privileged home than me and my family, I never thought any less of him. I was very open to new things and different people. Even though he was poor, small, black and did drugs, I saw more in him than most people did. He was also kind, considerate, loving, patient, ambitious and daring. He taught me so many things about life that I would never know today if not for him. He taught me things that made me more aware of the evils of this world and the people that live in it. Yes, he might be a grease monkey, but if not for him, I might not have survived the troubles of this world we live in today.

I was just now experiencing life and all it had to offer in the world outside of my own home and family parameters. Everything was interesting and intriguing. I was like a child in candy land. Eyes wide open seeing only the good and inviting things and not recognizing the bad when I saw it.

Wesley, me and a few of his friends – Fabian, Paulie, Junkie and Tall B would leave on Friday evenings, drive up to Toco in a couple of vehicles to spend weekends on the beach. No tents or anything, just food and drinks. Wesley and I usually fell asleep on the sand while looking up at the stars and listening to the waves wash the shoreline at the same time inhaling the salt air. The others just slept where they fell from too much weed and alcohol. It was heaven.

We all partied together at live band concerts at the yacht club and lots of other parties at various night clubs. My favorite was the Tempest Bar in the West Mall. It was a cozy joint.

I lived the typical privileged child lifestyle and enjoyed every minute of it. I was at war with my parents because of my relationship with Wesley. They saw what I couldn't yet they never did explain the reasoning behind it except for "do as we say and don't ask any questions!" Really, why? I was always the one that needed to ask 'why'. I know why now, now that it's way too late.

Three years after meeting Wesley, we discussed marriage. You must be wondering, what the heck was she thinking? He's a roadside mechanic from a poor background and she a privileged child with a good education and sound job. I saw nothing wrong with the equation. My father was a country boy that married the privileged white girl and all was well. I didn't know that I needed to take into account the family history of drugs and violence and the fact that Wesley had nothing but an elementary school education where my own father did graduate high school and came from a family of good morals and ethics. My own logic was limited and allowed me to make one of the worst mistakes of my life.

I then did something even more outrageous in deciding that I wanted to get pregnant before I got married. I was concerned that he might have suffered some physical damage to his loins from all his earlier years of drug use. I didn't want to get married and not be able to have children. This was just some stupid, reckless behavior from a spoilt girl. I can recognize that now and he with his street smarts used his masculine wiles to cloud my judgment anyway he could. This was something he could never dream would happen to him and he was not about to let it go. He had become the envy of all by having me as his girlfriend. He never knew such feelings.

Wesley and his family were not Trincity material. His family was poor and less privileged. They only lived there because his father tried to provide a more suitable home for his remaining children and bought that house for them some years after he moved to the US. They are originally from St. Babbs in Laventille, one of the worst areas in Trinidad. You did not want to find yourself there at anytime if you valued your life. There lived, amongst some simple, nice people, drug dealers, thieves, murderers and any other caliber of low life imaginable. He had lived there his entire life until just a few years before we met. He began smoking cigarettes when he was just 9 years old, dropped out of elementary school, then added weed, cocaine and crack to his drugs of choice as he aged. The perfect means to success as a seasoned junkie.

In November, 1985. I asked my mom, "Can Wesley spend the night?" I was already seven weeks pregnant and they knew it. Wesley did the right thing and told my mom as soon as we found out. She looked at me coldly and said, "No. You need to be married before that could happen under this roof." I had already moved into the maid's quarters by then. I was determined to move out of that house and gain my independence, but after a small battle, my father, who couldn't bear the thought of his darling daughter leaving, compromised. I would stay but in the maid's quarters since it was almost like a studio apartment except for the lack of a kitchen.

I looked at her just as coldly and flew into a silent rage. They would not allow me to grow up. I turned on my heels and marched out of the room, knowing what had to be done. The very next day I took the day off work, went with Wesley, Fabian and Paulie to the Red House and got married. Yes, so easy. I was dressed in a blue and white Capri, a white and blue tee with white sandals. Wesley wore jeans and tee shirt with his black, multi zipper vest (Michael Jackson styling) and his black converse sneakers. Fabian and Paulie wore jeans, jeans jackets, iron maiden tee shirts and cowboy boots. It must surely have looked to the clerk that this little black guy knocked up the little sister of these two big guys and they were making sure he did the right thing by her. It was a very comical situation. If marriage vows could have been any more screwed up than Wesley did them, I wouldn't believe it.

I don't think he was even speaking English yet he was supposed to be repeating what he was being told! We said our "I do's" and left, marriage certificate in hand. No celebration just went home. There were no pictures even of my happy day.

When I got home I dropped the marriage certificate in the center of my parents' bed and left. They were just outside the double glass doors of their room standing in the back yard. I could hear them talking quietly to each other. I listened for when they came into their bedroom and scuttled out front. Shortly afterwards I heard anxious words between them. I could hear my mother saying, "she got married." She sounded shocked. I couldn't make out what my dad was saying. I waited for them to come to me.

I sat outside on the front porch sitting on the wrought iron rocker rocking away and enjoying the cool breeze. It was a beautiful sunny day. Wesley was not there. He was only allowed there from 7PM even though I was already pregnant with his child. They both came out to me in full armor. I was ready. I sat there cool and stoic. I did not look at them until my mother spoke to me. "So you got married?" I turned my head slowly and looked at them both. "Yes." My dad looked shell shocked. He just couldn't say anything and was just staring at me eyes wide in disbelief. "Why didn't you tell us?" She continued. "You told me I needed to be married before Wesley could spend a night here. So, I'm married." "What?" My dad suddenly spoke. "You told her that?" "Yes, I did." My dad was appalled. "Why did you tell her that? Now look what she did!" My mom hung her head. She should have known better. My dad obviously knew what saying that to me would lead to. He was so angry with my mom at that moment. I sat there rocking and watching their exchange. "So, can Wesley spend the night now?" They looked at me, held their tongues and walked back inside toward their bedroom and closed the door.

Later that evening, my dad called me to sit with him. "Yuh mother and I have talked this over and Wesley can move in here wit you. You havin his child and is de right ting to do." I could not believe what I was hearing! I was ecstatic! I flung my arms around him. "Thanks Dad!" He hugged me looking so sullen like he had just lost his most precious belonging.

My pregnancy went by like a whirlwind. My coworkers catered to my every need and I was just gorgeous! My hair was so healthy and wavy and I simply radiated a glow that was like my own sunshine. They told me it was a boy because of that. Girls suck your beauty but boys turn you into a Goddess. I felt like a Goddess. Then the doctor told me I was diabetic and that I would need to watch my diet going forward. I was already six months along. No problem. I would do anything to make my child safe.

One month before the baby was due; the doctor said to me, "I'm going to have tuh induce labor. The baby is getting too big - unless it comes early. If nuthin by May 10, we will schedule the nearest date." The baby was actually due May 23. I was gung-ho. I was ready to get this baby out of me now for the past two months.

So, the delivery date was scheduled for May 13. I checked into Stanley's Maternity Clinic, a private facility on Maraval Road close to Port-of-Spain early the morning of May 13. It was a very nice place. Clean, professional and the nursing staff were awesome. Guess that's what you pay for at a private facility. This was all covered by my health insurance and I never took one penny out of my pockets. They had me undress and then took me to have an enema. That was a horrible experience. I was too young to even think that such procedures existed much less to experience them myself. Then around 1PM they set up the IV which would introduce the drug that would induce labor. After about two hours I began to experience pain like I've never imagined possible! Excruciating, crippling pain that made me wish I was dead rather than waiting to deliver a baby.

By 7PM that evening, I was weak from the pain, terrible contractions and no food. The doctor came by and since my water was yet to break, he decided he would snip the water bag with surgical scissors. The water flowed out of me warm and viscous. It felt like I was pissing on myself but not. It was a very weird feeling. At 9PM he came to see me. "I'm going to go home, but I will be back to deliver your baby, doh worry." I was nervous but understood he had his own family to get home to. I shook my head is acceptance while I couldn't hide the pain from my eyes. Wesley had already left around 8PM. He just couldn't take the pressure and needed to smoke more than wait for his first born.

At 11:30pm the nurses that had been checking on me every thirty minutes, came by and said that I was near ready. They called the doctor and while he was on his way they prepared me and transferred me to the delivery room. While I was still waiting for the doctor, the nurse was coaching and guiding me to my delivery. The doctor had not yet arrived when she said, "stop pushing." Was she kidding? You just had me pushing and now you say stop? She claimed to have seen the head. Luckily, the doctor arrived shortly thereafter looking like he just rolled out of bed, all disheveled and I swore he was wearing pajamas under his scrubs. It was now midnight.

He took over like a drill sergeant. He used a scalpel to cut my vaginal opening to avoid tearing and gave me some local anesthesia to ease the pain. There were no epidurals in those days. Then came the pushing. This was my first time doing this and I was not pushing like I should. He got upset with me and yelled at me to push as hard as I could. I did for at least three more times and then felt the unbelievable pain of the head and shoulders coming out of me. Everything else came out very easily. I was exhausted to the point of sleep. "It's a boy!" I heard in the distance. I remember they wrapped my son and placed him on my stomach facing me. His big dark blinking eyes looked at me. He was 8lbs. 10oz., chubby, light skinned with a full head of curly black hair. It was just me, him, the doctor and the nurse. His father had missed the entire thing. It was 12:38am on May 14. I fell asleep watching him, Adam Michel.

CHAPTER FIVE

The next few months were not very happy for me. Wesley and I fought like cat and dog. He spent a lot of time out of the home than in even though we had a newborn. He would take the baby in his stroller to hang out on the corner with him and his cronies while they smoked cigarettes, weed and anything else that was handy. I was foolish to think that he would have changed just because he was now a married man with a newborn son.

There was one time I packed all his belongings into three, black garbage bags. When he got home late that night, he didn't notice them at first, but when he did, he started laughing hysterically and said, "You putting me out?" He continued laughing while he got into the shower. He must have unpacked when he got out because when I awoke the next morning the bags were gone and his belonging returned to their usual place.

I returned to work after three months at home with my son. Wesley's mother, who lived only two streets behind us babysat for a fee. I just couldn't trust Wesley to take care of my son. He still didn't have a regular job and now with the added burden of baby expenses, I was feeling the financial strain. I began pressuring him to find a regular job.

This was a new realm for me. I've never had to budget anything. All that money that I used to have seemed to have evaporated. Adam was a problem child as well. He barely slept. He would sleep two hours then be up for two. I came to learn that this was a result of his father still doing cocaine when I became pregnant with him. I can recall Wesley assuring me that he had stopped all that stuff. What a bold faced lie that was! Now the child had mental problems.

Wesley got a couple of low paying jobs during the following months but he never stayed for more than a month at either. I was seeing the mistake I had made materialize in front of me. How was I going to fix this? On top of it all, my mother felt she could just intrude into our living space at any time. Sometimes I would awake at night to see her standing there holding my son. What the heck was that? No, I needed to do something and do it fast!

In March of 1987, when Adam was just 9 months old; I took a short vacation to the US to see my younger brother Gordon, who had been living in Rhode Island with our great aunt and uncle, Gloria and Clyde. I just needed a break from it all. I was gone for only ten days. It was heaven. In those ten days, Gordon encouraged me to move to the US. He said, "Why don't you move here? You would be able to live a better lifestyle than back home." I returned home thinking only of making such a move. Anything I thought would be better than what it was.

I spoke with Wesley and he was intrigued by the idea. He had never left Trinidad. I knew we couldn't go to Rhode Island as there would not be enough room for us all to live in my uncle's house. We called Wesley's father in New York. He tried to encourage me to have Wesley leave first, settle himself and then we could join him. First of all, Wesley didn't even have a passport. He did not have a bank account or a steady job which was mandatory for him to get a visa to travel. They expected me to work my magic and make it all happen for him and then wave goodbye to all my hard work. They must be mad! We all go or nobody goes! His father agreed to house us all when we arrive.

The decision made, I began putting things in place to exit the country. I was anxious for a better life. One month later, we were leaving. I resigned from my job after a steady rise to payroll teller in 1987.

I remember leaving Trinidad quite vividly. We spent our final days there living like a king and queen. We were chauffeured around and dined heartily at the Hilton Hotel, drank Dom Perignon champagne and enjoyed the small luxuries we indulged ourselves before we bade adieu to our home for the past twenty plus years. I was filled with excitement at the future we were about to embark upon. We were all packed, me, my husband and our 11 month old son and ready to go.

Piarco International Airport was busy as always. My parents and brother were there to see us off. Everywhere was bustling with excitement. I was literally jumping out of my pants just to get on the plane. Wesley held Adam while I checked us in and the bags. Then it was time to say our goodbyes and set off on our adventure. Had I known then what lay ahead of us I would not have been so anxious to leave. So young and full of life I was. My parents hugged me and Adam and wished us a good trip. I was surprisingly dry eyed throughout the entire exchange. In reality, I had my full family going with me so what was there to cry about? Little did I know at that moment the life of chaos and misery that lay ahead of us. I forged forward with wide opened eyes and a cheesy smile on my face.

It was mid afternoon and the flight was smooth and uneventful, all five hours of it. We arrived at John F. Kennedy International airport in New York City. Wesley's older brother Warren was expected to meet and bring us to where we were expected to stay until we found our own place. New York City; sounds exciting doesn't it? Yeah, I thought so too back then. I was clad in a red tee shirt that I stole from my youngest brother which read *Dazed and Confused*, pink tights and white sandals with my loser husband and sweet son similarly garbed at my side. Hey, I'd been travelling to the US since I was 12 years old, what's the big deal? You know what they say – see me and live with me is two different things. Yes, it is. I was young, daring and unstoppable. I came to this land with only $3,000USD that I got from selling my only possession, my Mazda, with my family in tow and thought everything would be just fine. What the hell did I know?? My 'husband', the 'roadside mechanic' that he's been so often called by my present 'beau' and actually is, knew even less!!

The date was April 11th, 1987. It was not quite warm yet and we didn't have any of the necessary clothing. Good thing for us NYC's weather is never very cold in April so we were still able to tolerate it. While I was composed and prepared to get started on building a new life, Wesley on the other hand was overwhelmed. I had taken the monkey out of the jungle and placed him into a concrete one. It was disastrous from day one.

Warren is a very nice guy; handsome, taller than Wesley and better spoken. I'd met him before when he visited Trinidad to see his mom and brothers and sister, so it was not an awkward meeting. "Y'all had a good flight?" Wesley answered with a nervous laugh, "huhmmm...yeah..." He was always intimidated by Warren for some reason unbeknownst to me. Warren helped with the luggage and we all headed out of the airport. I saw it all as if from virgin eyes like my son and husband did too. I've been here before many times yet not to stay. This was a whole different experience I didn't expect. We were filled with foolish excitement and anticipation. It should have been dread.

We were overcome by the enormity of the place and couldn't see the reality of the slum that it was. The first thing you do notice is the smell. The air is much different than in the islands, much different. It seemed to be a concoction of exhaust fumes, garbage, mold and mildew and stinky people. The roads are wide and heavily trafficked by speeding vehicles. Not like the two lane roads we were quite accustomed to back home. There are large apartment buildings everywhere, not simple residential one family homes like it is in Trinidad.

In Trinidad there may be the few townhouses that boasted at most two apartments and these were few and very far between. There was small talk between Wesley and Warren in the front seats while Adam and I sat in the back looking around like tourists at our new 'home' and taking it all in as we journeyed to our destination.

Warren took us back to his father's apartment on Nostrand Avenue just close to Beverly Road. Until recently, he had shared the apartment with him. It was a two bedroom, first floor apartment in a four floor, eight apartment building. Nostrand is no side street, it is a major road. Who would want to live on a major road in a building that houses a business at its front? There are various stores, laundromats, travel agencies and more at the front of almost all the buildings on that road! It is also a major bus and NYC subway train route with the 2 and 5 Flatbush Avenue trains running along underground with a stop just at the corner of our 'block' on Beverly Rd. This must be what it's like to live in Port-of-Spain maybe? It became 'home' for about six months.

My father-in-law, Claude was a real piece of work. Left his wife, two sons and daughter in Trinidad and came to NYC in 1968 with his first three sons. At the time he arrived, America was the 'apple' of the entire world. Everybody wanted a piece! After 19 years, he was still living in a rinky dink apartment, had no credit and no new wife but many girlfriends. He suffered the typical male syndrome of "being God's gift to women". He didn't know about women in America but he found out. He did have a dog though. One that I saw him attempt to drown in the bathtub when it disobeyed him. What a psycho he was.

I remember standing at the bathroom door, watching the dog sit in the tub while Claude loomed over him with his hands around its neck. I watched as the animal cried and looked up into the eyes of his beloved owner terrified and confused and not knowing what the heck was going on! The poor animal was helpless and so was I to offer any help. The man looked crazed, his eyes bulging out of his head, shouting unrecognizable words while dunking the dog under the water in the bathtub that continued to fill. I felt like I was watching a scene in a bad movie. As suddenly as he began his assault it ended. He released the poor dog from his impending tomb. Shutting the water off, he grabbed a towel from the towel rack and began to dry the dog and whisper sweet soft words to him. I stepped away and went to my room in a daze. What kind of animal was this man? Till this day I don't understand what the dog could have done to deserve what he got.

The apartment was infested with roaches – millions to be fair and just as many mice. Claude would set traps everywhere for the mice and roast them on the stove when he caught them. Yes, he did that! He enjoyed watching them squeal and try to escape the flames of death to no avail. It was just not a habitable environment.

Besides exhibiting this psychotic behavior he was also attempting to woo me away from his son. Believe it or not! I was again reminded of the huge mistake it was coming to the US!! My husband was swept away by the glitz and glamour. A 'roadside mechanic' could find work easily in NYC. Laborers could get paid 'under the table' which meant not on the books and earn tax free income illegally. So called professionals like myself could not.

During our first few months here, my brother paid for me and Adam to fly to Rhode Island to visit him. It was a nice break from the chaos in New York. While there, he took me to get my driver's license. At that time all that was needed was for me to show my foreign license and take a multiple choice test on the computer. I was even able to get the actual license right away, not like today when it comes in the mail two weeks later! Gordon told me that after six months I can go to the department of motor vehicles in New York and exchange it for a NY license. After a few days we returned to New York.

By August, I found myself in an even worse predicament. My husband, came 'home' from one of his routine escapades one night, drunk and out of control, forced himself on me, not even bothering to wake me and a few weeks later I was pregnant. Of course, my sisters-in-law, Elaine, Warren's girlfriend, who couldn't conceive and the other Nancy whose man, Steve, senior to Warren was just a rogue, never once advised me of the free medical and contraceptive care I could have received from Kings County Hospital that was literally walking distance from where we lived! How could Wesley be so irresponsible?? We did not even have our own place yet for Christ's sakes!

Wesley was just enjoying life. It was his first time anywhere away from life as he's known it for his 26 years and he was loving it! I, on the other hand, was suffering along with my son.

I am a black woman, but my hair and skin color does not depict it. My mother was Irish/Lebanese and my father some French/Hispanic type of mutt, thus I look white. Tall, light brown/blond hair, light brown eyes, Madonna like figure and facial features very similar to that of an Egyptian Goddess. A young, vibrant beauty, totally naïve and new to the land, I was prime cut bait! Women hated me, men loved me yet everybody wanted to be my friend. I was 21, living in a predominantly black neighborhood, which by the way, made no difference to me since all around me were islanders like myself, and was clueless to the racism that surrounded me. Why would I think about racism? I was among people that came from where I did? They weren't white. I never was exposed to anything called racism until I came to America.

I didn't know it then but came to learn that my sisters-in law were jealous of me and that explained why they wouldn't help me. Was it my fault that their men were enthralled by my beauty? I didn't want their men. They provided meager handouts in the forms of clothing for my son and some government subsidized food stuffs they may have lined up for at a shelter somewhere. As black people proudly say, 'if it's free it's for me!'

I believe they took some sadistic pleasure in seeing me suffer as a result of Wesley's street walking and not taking care of his family. It allowed them to look the heroines to someone who in reality considered their own existence as meaningless! I was just too naïve. I came from my father's house to this zoo. I was totally unprepared and unarmed for the future that was to come.

What have I done? I asked myself over and over again. I could not tell my parents or family the hell I was in. I got married for better or for worse and there was nobody that I could point to that might have forced me to give up a great bank job and comfortable life in my own country. I needed to deal with my own issues and I would. Now I can see that I did not make the right decisions or choices, but with nobody advising me or let's say giving me the right advice, I went down the rocky and thorny path to where I am today. I made my bed and now I lay in it.

CHAPTER SIX

I was six months into my pregnancy when we moved to a house on East 35th Street. Wesley never once mentioned we were moving before that day. One crisp, fall day, he arrived home from work with some extra large, black garbage bags and started packing the few possessions we had. He said, "We're movin outta here today." He had obviously been thinking of this moment all day long I surmised. I had no idea what had caused this sudden decision nor did I care. I wanted out of that place probably more than he did.

We proceeded to pack all our measly belongings into the ten year old Volvo he had bought a couple of months ago for chump change. The car was registered and insured in my name using my New York license. This became yet another nightmare to deal with that I've never before experienced. We drove off into the sunset toward our next adventure. Wesley drove everyday to and from work and everywhere else with no driver's license. New York was now just an extension of Trinidad for him. He was basically settled in.

By then, I was accustomed to the erratic behavior. He was mad and I knew it. I was stuck with him. What type of place was it that he heroically took his family to you ask? It was a room, yes, and a large room in a filthy, broken down house owned by Haitian immigrants. They had found a good niche for financial opportunity. They bought houses and rented them it out by rooms to make extra income. Our room's rate was $350 a month and it would have been the living room if the house was as it should have been. The place was disgusting! The kitchen and bathroom was public to all tenants and their guests. Not a sanitary or healthy environment for a pregnant woman and her infant son, but what did he know or care?

We slept on the floor of our 'new home' that night. Me, six months pregnant and my 18 month old son slept on a dirty, smelly old carpet that was the only thing left there from the previous tenants. It was just another room in hell for me. Different floor same building; I was moving up in the world. I thought I had seen roaches in the previous place but I hadn't seen anything until here. This was the mother load of all roaches, I was sure of it! We could never get rid of them, never! Of course, the mice were there too. I felt sure we were supposed to be renting from these pests instead. They behaved as though we were encroaching on their turf and should just leave!

It was there that I met Leti. Leti was a Mexican immigrant who was married to a Haitian cab driver that lived in the room next to ours on the first floor. Leti had mega problems with that man and they had a two year old daughter named Stephanie that was out of control. He was a bum and she was frustrated ultimately leaving him a couple of years later. We totally bonded. It was Leti that told me about Kings County Hospital and about how I could get the free prenatal care I so desperately needed. It's a country where a stranger would help you before a friend or family member. She was a good friend and I wish we had stayed in touch. She ran out of there like a bat outta hell leaving no trace of her existence behind.

As soon as humanly possible, I took my son and off we went to Kings County Hospital. The people there were very helpful and that was a time when immigrant status did not affect the medical privileges you were allowed. When it was my turn to see the doctor and explain my situation he was appalled! My bloodwork revealed that I was terribly anemic. It was a bad situation. Along with prenatal vitamins, the doctor also prescribed iron supplements three times a day which I needed to continue until three months after the birth of my daughter in May, 1988. Thankfully, the hospital pharmacy provided me all at no cost. I continued receiving medical care there since it was just walking distance from my home. I will never forget Leticia for the help she gave me.

My precious daughter Danni was almost born at home. Why? As usual, my street walker husband was not home until midnight on May 20th! The night before that I went to visit my childhood friend Anne-Marie who was moving to Canada the next day. She lived in an apartment building on Rockaway Parkway just off Kings Highway. When we were leaving after our visit, I slipped on the staircase. There was heavy rainfall that day and the floors and stairs were wet. I was holding Adam's hand to help him down the stairs since the stairs were pretty deep.

Her place was on the top floor and there was no elevator. The stairs were marble tile and I didn't notice the small puddle that had collected there. I was holding Adam's hand and started on my way down. I was literally nine months pregnant!! I slipped on the top stair. I went down fast and pulled my son's head directly into the stair rail in the process.

His head hit hard!! I let him go instantly and allowed myself to continue sliding down the stairs on my ass. All I could think about was my son. Was he ok? He was sitting on the floor, red faced and screaming at the top of his lungs. At the same moment, Wesley came running up the stairs. He had come to get us. He looked me dead in my eye as I was still sliding down the stairs and quickly turned around and went back down without even looking back. I picked up my son who was miraculously ok and went down to the car. Wesley said nothing. As we drove home I began to experience sharp abdominal pains. They eventually subsided but never totally went away. This was May 19th, 1988.

The next day I was officially in labor. I lost my 'plug' at 7:30pm on May 20. I was home alone with Adam as was the usual case. Day merged into night and soon it was midnight. I was sitting on the steps outside the house wondering what the hell I was going to do. My contractions were now twenty minutes apart and getting more and more intense. Adam just turned two last week and was of course sleeping. Here he came; pulls up in front of the house, with his friend Arthur in the car and music blasting. "What are you doing sitting there?' he asked. "I need to go to the hospital right away." I looked him squarely in his eyes. "Yuh ready?" I said to him, "You don't plan on leaving Adam here sleeping do you?" "No, wake him up." I began shaking my head, "No. Leh Arthur take meh to de hospital." Anyways, Arthur was the one that took me to the hospital. He kept asking me stupid questions on the way there, one the likes of "how do you know you're having the baby?" Thank goodness it was only a five minute drive away.

When we arrived at the hospital I jumped out of the car and hurried inside the emergency room entrance on Clarkson Avenue. I walked like a crooked old woman, holding my stomach and hunched over walking with my legs spread apart. "I'm in labor!" I moaned. A nurse hurriedly brought a wheel chair and I gently lowered myself onto it. I was taken to a waiting room where I was transferred to a gurney. When the nurse finally came about ten minutes later to check how far I was dilated, I was in the middle of a contraction and simply could not open my legs. She got snippy when I explained to her that I couldn't open my legs just then and left in a huff. I could not believe it. This is the city hospital which is probably the same caliber of the General Hospital, aka, the Disco in Trinidad.

I knew the baby was coming and I was not in the delivery room. The nurse eventually came back and was able to examine me. I opened my legs. "Stop pushing!" she screamed. "I'm not pushing!" I yelled back. She said, "I can see the head right there!" All hell broke loose after that. They scrambled to transfer me to another gurney and quickly get me across the hall to a delivery room.

By the time I got in there, placed my feet in the stirrups, the doctor situated herself in front of me and hollered "PUSH!" I gave it one hard push and felt a huge weight released from my body. The relief is an amazing feeling right at that moment. My baby girl was delivered on May 21 at 4:38am, Danni Desiré. The baby came before they were ready and tore me from front to back, twenty-one stitches! I almost broke the doctor's finger when she started stitching me up. I was anesthesia free remember. Her thumb turned blue immediately; it was too bad. My beautiful, ET looking baby was born and nobody was happy, not her, not me. What was there to be happy about? What?

The days that followed the birth of my daughter are still too painful to put into words but I will try. When it was time to leave the hospital three days later, Wesley showed up to get us from the hospital, arms swinging. The nurse on call looked at him incredulously. "You didn't bring any clothes for your wife or the baby to go home? You're wearing a jacket; you don't think they need clothes to leave here? We will not let them leave until they are appropriately dressed." She turned her back to him and looked at me questioningly. She was Jamaican and tough. I could only hang my head and look at the floor. That look said all that I already knew. It said, *"Are you sure you know what you're doing with this man? Cause I think you've made a big mistake here!"* No I wasn't sure and I thought that same thing every day that I woke to see the morning. I cradled Danni, sat on my hospital bed and waited for Wesley to return with hopefully appropriate clothing because I couldn't face another round of embarrassment.

When he returned, what he had was ample to allow us exit from the hospital. The nurse made sure she checked what he brought and kept looking at him seemingly amazed that he was actually the husband and father in this equation. She was not the only one that had such questions. Most everyone did. I was relieved to leave and just get my baby home to our already overcrowded room.

Danni would use Adam's crib. It was missing a few bars from its attack by the previous resident, but it would have to do. I used pillows to cover the spaces so she won't accidentally fall out. We had added a bunk bed to the room for Adam. The room now had a wardrobe, full sized bed, the bunk bed, a normal sized crib, a single chair that was once part of a living room set, a four drawer dresser on top of which sat the 19" television and a baby changing table that was used to store Adam's clothes and anything else that needed somewhere to sit. Imagine how much space we had to move around. Imagine how much space a two year old had to run around.

We got home five minutes later and I couldn't wait to just get inside. I was running a small fever and the child needed to feed. I never was able to produce ample milk from my breasts for the babies so it was formula all the way. I got inside, undressed and placed Danni in the crib and then got undressed myself. I looked around for the formula and bottles. There weren't any. I looked at Wesley, "Where are the baby formula and the bottles? You were supposed to get them." "Oh, I didn't get it yet." I turned on him sharply, hurting myself slightly in the process. "What?" I couldn't believe it! "So how am I supposed to feed the baby now?" "Wey yuh does get dem tings?" I sat down as my knees could no longer support me. "I doh know Wesley. Sears……any bargain store." I had provided him with exactly what items to get to make sure everything was right for when the baby came home. Yet, all was wrong! I held my son who had sorely missed me and looked at the poor child in the crib. She was crying. It appeared to me that she knew she was not welcome. She cried so softly that even with everything still in the room you could barely hear her. It seemed like she just didn't want to be a burden and was sorry that she was here.

That moment, was the first time my heart stirred for this child. I didn't want her from day one. I felt such guilt at what she must have felt during the nine months I carried her. Now I looked at her innocent, sweet face as she lay in the crib crying softly. I picked her up and cradled her while I planted soft kisses on her face. "It's going to be ok sweetheart. I promise everything will be alright." I didn't sound convincing even to myself. Suffice it to say, the end of my so called marriage was now in its secondary stage.

When you think things couldn't get any worse, they did! How much hell can one person stand? What did I ever do to deserve this? I was a good girl, with a sound upbringing and education who never hurt anyone but has been abused and violated her entire life. When was life going to get easier? Was I suffering the sins of my parents, grandparents or great grand parents? So now I had two children. Sobering and confusing for an innocent like myself. I felt like I was chasing my own tail, spinning in circles and getting nowhere, at least nowhere good.

We stayed in that one room until Danni was at least 3 and Adam almost 5! My parents visited that year. I was so embarrassed for them to see how and where I lived. When they got there, they pretended not to notice my horrible living conditions and never mentioned it after. They had spent some time in Rhode Island, and then came to New York on their way to New Jersey to stay with my mom's older brother and my Godfather, Uncle Tommy. It was Christmas time, so that helped distract me from the horrors of my shame.

It was the last time I saw my mother alive. I wish I had known what was to come; I would have tried to mend the rift between us then. It remained firmly in place for the following eight years of our lives unresolved until her death.

Then, one day, we moved again. Same moving style like the last, except this was to an actual apartment. Yay! Our own bathroom and kitchen! I came to appreciate more the simple things in life. Granted, it was a small, one bedroom on Church Avenue just off 53rd Street, but it was better than where we were ten times over. For those that don't know Church Avenue is an even worse road than Nostrand Avenue! It is a main route for at least two different subway stations and was a major shopping avenue. There were hundreds of gypsy cabs (illegally operated taxis, usually driven by unlicensed, illegal immigrants) and the B35 bus route. Church Avenue never slept. It was the link to many other bus and train routes. A major hub you could say.

We were in the back apartment with another in front on the top floor of a business owned and occupied by the landlord. During the time before this move, we took small driving trips to Rhode Island, Virginia Beach and Massachusetts many times visiting my brother and his family in RI, vacationing in VA and spending time with Wesley's welfare receiving, drug dealing cousins in Mattapan, Massachusetts! Hey, it was all new and different to me and interesting in my otherwise boring, fruitless life! Kinda like living a movie life, a ghetto hood movie that is, but still one nonetheless.

Claude approached us on one of our 'family' visits to his home. He asked what it would take for him to help us get our green cards. I was immediately intrigued and excited. That week, I went to the Brooklyn Public Library and researched the necessary steps to achieve our goal. According to the laws, since Wesley was over 25 and married, his father needed to be a citizen of the United States in order to proceed. That would need to be the first order of things.

Wesley was able to get his first and only driver's license in Massachusetts. All that was needed was someone to vouch for you that had one. Massachusetts followed its own laws. It is a commonwealth state as is Virginia. His cousin took him down, he did the computer test and passed and then scheduled the driving test for the next available date. He also passed that test when the time came.

I had never in my life been exposed to such environments or situations as with Wesley's cousins in Massachusetts. I was intrigued. I was a Catholic school girl for Christ's sakes. What the hell did I ever experience or witness but some Trini versioned white girls smoking in the school bathroom or trying to get laid by the only male teacher in the school? Regular stuff. That was when my own cheating days started. A little over the so-called seven year mark they usually give you. What was a woman to do? I had needs that weren't being satisfied and not only sexually. I was emotionally and intellectually starved!

I enjoyed cheating. It's shameful to say but I did and I was good at it too. I hang my head in shame today at some of the things I lowered myself to do and experience. I was raised better than that. I was also very, very lost. I won't make any excuses for my lurid behavior. The reasons were there. I confided in my sisters-in-law and they encouraged me. Ignorance is bliss, especially in America, a land full of the blissfully ignorant! My shenanigans and escapades continued for many years being my escape from reality. Cheating for me was a mastered art. Anything worth doing.....is worth doing well. It was worth it for me at the time. I had my pick of the crop, from fellow Trinis, to Jamaicans, to Afghanis, to Irish, to Italian, to Dominicans to Haitians; to Americans and of course Africans. I apologize now to all that I offend with this piece. It's my story.

CHAPTER SEVEN

Two miscarriages later, my children were 7 and 5 and were both in school fulltime. Still on Church Avenue and tired of the empty life I had had it! It was now seven years since we first arrived in this country and nothing had resulted in respect to the legitimacy of our immigrant status. We had given up on Wesley's father sponsoring us as alien relatives. I'm sure it's no surprise when I tell you he was still only a resident alien at the time of our arrival and till his death a few years ago. What a waste, of effort and time! This was just ignorant, West Indian lack of common sense.

During the period when we were pursuing his citizenship, it was my charter to take him around to get his fingerprints, help fill out the application forms and whatever else would put us together so he could work on getting his citizenship done in order to help us. Then one day, we were standing in front of his house, yes he finally bought a house after being in America for 25 years, on Sackman Street in Brownsville (one of the worst areas in Brooklyn by the way), me, Wesley, and the kids, when he turned to me and said, "Why are you even with him anyways? Why don't you just move in with me?" That day was the last time we ever saw that old man, at least for another five years! His son made sure of it. The insult and the effrontery of the man!

Time began dragging on again with no positive future to look forward to. Something had to happen, it just had to. I felt like a wild bird trapped in a cage and I was dying. My spirit was stained and my freedom eluded me far too long. I needed to do something, and then, a ray of hope. During all the drama of my life, my best friend Sue from the bank back in Trinidad had moved to New York. She lived in Jamaica, Queens, where almost all the people of East/West Indian descent live in NY. I don't know why so don't expect any explanation. She knew someone who could help get a work permit. He said the fee would be $300USD. He claimed it was legitimate however years later I understood it could not have been. I was trying to make some money on the side by selling Mary Kay products and with this cause at hand, you can bet your bottom dollar I was able to get that money!

It took three weeks to get the work permit back from the guy who looked like an oversized rat pretending to be human. Kinda like Splinter from Teenage Mutant Ninja Turtles. It was always difficult not to laugh at him when he was around. I was still a girl at heart and very playful, what can I say. Don't condemn me please. I took that work permit directly to the Social Security office; me with my two babies in tow. I was determined and there was nothing and no one that was going to stop me. Nothing did. It was infallible and I received my social security card in the mail within two weeks at my home.

Sue had received her own some months before and was already working so she directed me to the agency she had signed up with and that's exactly where I went. I tested and started working a couple weeks later. They were great people. I did one temp assignment and then landed a long term one in December of 1995 that ended up becoming a permanent job for me for the next five years!! I was working as a front desk receptionist at eleven dollars an hour and loving it! Things were finally picking up. I saw a light at the end of the tunnel. I thought the dark cloud had dissipated and sunshine would clear away all my pain and heartache.

I began to make plans for a better future. Maybe now that I was working I would be able to save some money and one day get my own place. Well, that was more stupidity on my part. That good old naïveté again. Wesley had his own plans for me. He was always sure that I would leave him if I ever started working and he was seeing his nightmare materialize right before his eyes. He was not going to allow that to happen at all! It's that old adage, if I can't have you nobody else will! He said that to me many times too! His plan was simple, I now needed to contribute to the household, pay some bills and buy some food. Mind you, I was only working part-time even though it was five days a week. He made sure that I would have nothing to put aside and being the fair minded person I am, I felt he was not wrong to expect me to contribute to the home. After all, he was 'taking care' of it for the past years all by himself so why shouldn't he expect some alleviation off his burdened shoulders? Another road block. Dammit!

Some poor delusional fool told me many years later that having kids would concretize a relationship. What a load of crock! I had two and my relationship was in the tank. I was so ready to bail it was not even funny. Kids make no difference when the relationship sours. I know that for an actual fact based on experience. So that idea rolled off me like water off a ducks' back.

There was nothing to put aside, absolutely nothing. I was barely able to buy myself some affordable, decent looking professional clothes. What I mean is - cheap! I was working in corporate America you know. Still, I was awarded some freedom from my cage and it made it all worthwhile. I stayed out late many times going out drinking with my co-workers. It helped and I took advantage of any freedom I could get.

Needless to say, things got worse, if that's even fathomable by you. I pretty much lived as though I was a single parent. It was made easy since the other part of the equation was practically nonexistent in the home. Tertiary stage of dissolution was pretty much in effect at this point. Wesley was almost never home. By the time he got in from his street walking we were all asleep and he left very early every morning for work. We definitely were in the eye of the storm and it was peaceful. It was very easy to pretend soon after, that he really didn't even exist. I mastered that one well. I really can't explain how, you have to do it yourself to know.

My home was truly dysfunctional in every aspect. My children were suffering right before my eyes and I was impervious to their needs. I was so happy to have some sort of peace from the hell I'd been living that I didn't want to think hard at all. I just wanted to enjoy life and live a little. I didn't know what the heck I was doing. It's plain and simple. This is where I went so far off course that I am still paying for it today.

Adam soon began exhibiting dysfunctional behavior in school which began when he was in the 2nd grade at age 7, and has continued till today. He will be 23 in May of next year.

I was always in the school answering some teacher's call or another. "Your son is disruptive in class." "Your son is fighting with this or that one." Your son stuck a pencil in this one's hand." The worse was, "Your son brought a gun to school." What? Yes, a silver, 22 caliber cigarette lighter that his father felt was something cool to have. That one took him to disciplinary court and he was suspended for two weeks. They then told me it would be best to enroll him into the special education program where he would get more attention in a smaller classroom setting. I knew he responded well to one-on-one interaction so I agreed. He was scheduled to see the school counselor twice a week until further notice.

Despite all their lamentations, his grades were excellent up until this point. The boy simply had a brain that was fast; too fast for his own good. They even had me take him to a NY State psychiatrist for evaluation at Kings County hospital. Funny thing is, the state psychiatrist told me just what I knew was 'wrong' with the boy – he's just a boy is all. I knew it!

The experience was too much for the child. He developed social and self confidence issues. His grades dropped drastically. It was a crying shame. This was a child that could read fluently before he even started school at the age of five and when I say fluently, there was no word that he couldn't read or say, even if he didn't know its meaning! I had been home schooling him while we were home together in his earlier years.

Danni just never 'got' school and I never even noticed how bad it was until she was in the ninth grade! What does that tell you? How bad a mother I was? Maybe. I always knew she was a little slow but she could do hair like a professional at age nine! If she could use her hands, she could make a living. I was not worried about her at all. She had a gift. Danni never experienced the luxury of having me home school her because by the time she came along and was ready for school I was in a very bad place emotionally and totally inept. I also started to work as soon as she started full day school. She was a good girl though and never got into any trouble in school.

My poor children. I keep asking myself, what have I done? Why does it need to be this hard for immigrants in this country? We aren't thieves or murderers, at least not the majority of us. We're simply educated people whose own country didn't afford the opportunities as this one did. We simply want our children to have a good life. We wanted a piece of the American pie!

CHAPTER EIGHT

I was working now and feeling good about myself. I had friends; I was doing what I wanted when and how I wanted. Life was good or as good as it could get. That was so very far from the truth it's just not funny. Not funny at all. I continued along that thorny, rocky path and made yet another choice that kept me there for the next 10 years!

I was so enjoying corporate life in NYC! My friends at work were awesome and I must say some have remained my friends to this very day! It was a software development firm for the financial industry, mainly banks so I was in my true realm. I was very comfortable with bankers and IT professionals. Life was becoming sweet once more. Well, sweet at work anyways. Always was the dreaded trip home. I looked forward to seeing my children every evening but not to my home and the environment we were living in. I knew I wasn't going to be able to change it anytime soon and saw no way out of the situation. The kids appeared happy. They were younger anyways. What did they know? I needed to find some outlet for my frustrations and eventually did….sitting on the corner right by my home every day.

He was young, vibrant and intriguing to me. I watched and studied him every day. Every blink, turn of the head, how he moved, how he spoke, how he expressed himself, but what intrigued me the most was that he appeared to need no one. He was usually alone and seemed lost in thought. I didn't know then he was just always high from smoking weed.

Never loud and obnoxious and very polite and totally shy! I had my mark and went in for the kill. He'll probably hope to have my head on a platter if he reads this, but so what, we're way past that chapter in our lives. I began to look forward to the trip home.

Generally, I would stay out on the sidewalk on afternoons and weekends so as to allow the kids to be able to play freely (run up and down the busy sidewalk). Apartment life in New York City is very restrictive, with no back yards or porches it's truly a difficult way to raise healthy children. He usually sat outside the corner store which was literally three doors away from my own. The store was owned by Jamaicans who continuously played loud reggae music all day and night which attracted the unemployed, underprivileged and otherwise lazy asses to sit and loiter around!

He was adorable. Light skinned black, short dreadlocks, just growing out, like a bob, about 5' 9'' and maybe 160lbs with the cutest button nose. He looked to be in his early 20's and his name is Russell. I just turned 30 so that's not too bad…is it? Well I didn't think so at the time.

One day I was paying for something in the store and he came in to get a beadie (a small hemp cigarette). He stood right next to me waiting for me to finish. I looked at him and he turned to look at me. I smiled and said, "Hi" He said "Hi" and turned his attention back to the man behind the counter. I took my change from the man and with a pencil from the counter, wrote my pager number on a one dollar bill and gave it to Russell. "Call me." He beamed and said a hearty, "Thank you!" and proceeded to spend the dollar bill even before I got out of the store.

I was so embarrassed. This was the first time I was ever so forward with a man and for this little unemployed street bum to do me like that was heart breaking. I held my head high when he exited the store with the candy bar and soda that he bought for himself with my dollar bill. I was still outside with the kids and looked at him as he happily ate and drank whilst he looked at me with a greedy grin on his face. Ok, I thought to myself. You get this round.

Another opportunity presented itself pretty soon after that. As I said, he was always outside that store with his friends and acquaintances. One night, I was at a party around the corner – at my friend Vickie's, and we ran out of ice. She and I decided to go to the store together. I was dying to show her who I had my eyes on and I knew for certain he would be there. It was around 11:30pm on a Saturday night.

Sure enough, he was sitting outside the store with only one of his friends, one called LP. LP was a womanizer. Cute, little, light browned dreadlocks kid with a buoyant personality, about 19 or so. He had tons of girls after him. He was extremely loud too. I was dressed in a very short black dress with low heels. I was made up for party night. Vickie and I were also a little bit tipsy; we had been partying since nine o'clock.

I made eye contact with him as we entered the store and held it as I moved into the doorway. He didn't look away. I smiled an inviting smile and said, "Hi" It's comical, but I saw his eyebrows jumping all over his face. I had obviously made him nervous. Strike two for me. I hadn't realized that I had also enthralled LP with that smile. They were both looking up at me and couldn't look away. Then LP said to Russell, "Who's that? Is that that kid's mother?" Everybody knew Adam. You don't know how many times I pulled him out from between all those guys in the arcade around the corner, just under the cloud of cigarette and marijuana smoke. He just never listened.

Vickie and I kept giggling and chatting in the store. "He's cute, Debbie." "You think so?" "YES!" More giggling. "Give him your number again. On a piece of paper this time!" Giggle I wrote my pager number again on the receipt. We got the ice and upon leaving both said bye to the boys in unison giggling some more. I placed the receipt directly in his hands at that time, number side up. Their stares followed us to her car as we entered and drove off. They looked very amused by the entire exchange. I knew I had broken the shell. I now needed to sink my hook in deeper and reel him in. I later came to find out that he was Guyanese by birth, 22 years old but more importantly, was a naturalized US citizen since he was 6.

He called me the following Tuesday. I usually left for work at 10:30am to get there for Noon. I took a gypsy cab on Utica Avenue to Eastern Parkway and then took the 4 subway train to Bowling Green where I worked. He called at 8:30am. Everyone in the area knew our schedules. It was a neighborhood like that. It looked too busy but it was full of busy bodies. He knew Wesley was not there.

My pager had voicemail and I became overly excited when I heard his voice on the message. The number was not familiar to me and I didn't know who it was before checking the message. He wanted to come over. I called the number he left and when he answered, I told him he could come over in thirty minutes. I needed to freshen up and tidy the place first! After forty minutes and no Russell, I called again and he explained that he'd developed sudden stomach problems. I knew he was nervous and I knew how to fix that. "Don't worry then. We could always hook up some other time." The lack of pressure made for a miraculous recovery. He was ringing the door bell within three minutes.

I tried not to run down the stairs to open the front door. I needed to keep my cool. I opened the door and he darted quickly inside I guess to avoid being noticed. It was early morning on a weekday. He ran up the stairs ahead of me and I quickly followed. I locked the apartment door behind us and followed him into the living room. "Sit." My outstretched arm directed him to the sofa. I plopped down next to him.

He sat nervously, fingers entwined, legs closed tightly together, furiously pumping up and down. Didn't he know that showed me he was nervous? The innocence of youth. It's quite refreshing.

"So", I began, as I sat with my body turned toward his and very close, "What made you decide to call me afterall?" He shrugged his shoulders and gave an *I dunno* expression. "Well I'm glad you did call and came. How's yuh stomach?" "Better." "Oh good." I began touching his arm then his leg while chatting about nothing really. I was working my magic on parts of him he thought he was in control of right there and then. I stopped talking and leaned in to kiss him on the mouth. He readily conceded still maintaining his rigid poise. I continued kissing him while my hands explored under his shirt and then the front of his pants. I was pleased to feel what I expected. A rigid and ready tool for my use. "Let's go to the bedroom." I led him to the bedroom and laid on the bed. He laid on top of me still kissing me. I quickly removed my panties and when he saw the prize that awaited him, his pants came off in seconds.

I was anxious to feel him slide into me. His rod was stiff and beautiful. Big, caramel colored, swollen and glowing with the vibrance of youth. He retrieved a condom from his pants pocket that looked too old to be of any use. This kid must not engage in too much sex I thought to myself. I touched his hands and pushed it away. He threw it aside and sunk his penis into my ready and waiting hole. It was one of the sweetest sexual episodes I've ever experienced. Twenty minutes later when he was leaving, I knew this was not the end of this. "See you." I said and closed the door. I don't think I heard his response if there was one.

I quickly got ready for work and ran toward Utica Avenue. As I was crossing the street, I looked at him as he sat with his friend around the corner. He looked spent and satisfied. He even seemed shocked for some reason. Maybe he didn't expect the treasure he received. By his expression, I knew I had him right where I wanted him.

Then followed my true spiral downturn into the abyss of fornication, alcohol and drugs. Yeah. This was the escape from reality I was looking for. It was awesome. I was spiritually dying at my own accord and enjoying every minute of it! Yeah, life felt good finally! Foolish woman!

This young man allowed me to feel young at heart again. I started to feel alive and like a vibrant woman all over again. I wasn't just "their mother" or "his wife". I became Debbie and I was in charge of this shit! I began to escape that darkness that shrouded me. Light was everywhere. I was working, playing and loving life. You know what the really sad thing was? My children enjoyed life with me, even if it was wrong! Together, we went everywhere and played a lot, like a parent should with a kid. Life was good for everyone. I could say that then, not now.

I was slowly ruining my children's lives and my own in all my frolicking. They were being taught to disrespect people. They learned the ways of a cheating wife and mother. They knew of an absent father. They learned what it was like to be neglected from the true nurturing of a mother and father. I never cared to check their homework. They were grown enough to be responsible I told myself and I was enjoying life too much to bother. Never did I realize that they were taking advantage of the situation. They didn't do their homework and were also getting involved in things they should not be involved in outside of the home!

This frolicking went on for two good years! I saw this as a means to an ultimate end. I intended to use this relationship to perhaps gain my green card. I just needed to find the right time and words to broach the subject with Russell. The way I saw it, what did he have to lose?

During that time, Wesley and I had briefly separated for about five months. One day, while we were driving to McDonald's on Utica and Clarkson Avenues, I took the chance. He was driving. "Russell..." "Uummm?" He was looking at the road. "Do you think you might be able to help me get my green card?" Without looking at me and seeming not surprised by the question he said, "How? Marry you?" "Yes." I was looking at him the entire time trying to gauge his reactions to everything. He turned into the drive-thru lane of McDonald's and drove up to the order window. "One chicken nugget and one cheeseburger happy meal; two number 10's (fish sandwich meal), HiC fruit punch with the happy meals and one medium sprite and one medium coke!" I shouted over him to the speaker. The person inside said "$18.64. Drive around please." We drove to the pick-up window.

While we waited on them to bring the food, he looked at me and said, "Some lady asked me to do that for her before. When I told my Mom she told me that people pay up to $5,000 for that." I just looked at him, a little surprised by the response. After a few seconds, I responded. "Well I have no money to give you, so......" He never mentioned it again until years after Raven was born. Neither did I.

I thought long and hard about the exchange while I lay in bed later that night. What did I expect? Where did you find him anyways? On the corner. So what type of character would you expect him to have? I usually paid for everything wherever we went since he was jobless so why won't he look to make a quick buck out of me? I felt beaten. My diabolical plan backfired right into my face.

This was plan A since Plan B would be to wait until Danni turned 21 to petition for me as her 'alien relative'. Manipulating and molding him was enjoyable work, but work nonetheless. I didn't believe at this point that continuing on this path would be beneficial for me. I decided to just wait and see how things pan out. I had bigger problems right then. I was being evicted because Wesley hadn't paid the rent for the five months prior to our separation and the courts gave me six months to leave so basically I had one month left to find a place.

I was back at square one. I was still married to Wesley and didn't have the money for a divorce and wasn't really sure of how it's done since we were married back in Trinidad. There was another way, plan C; and that was employment sponsorship. That's if your employer agreed to petition for you as an 'alien worker'. Note the derogatory terms used by the US Immigration and Naturalization Service. This was a long and drawn out process that was not guaranteed. That was not an option for me until a few years later. Marriage to a US citizen was the easiest and fastest route. You could get your green card within six months to one year. I took a step back and spent some time reassessing the relationship without giving him any indication that I was dejected and insulted by his response.

Wesley hadn't given up trying to come back home which I found ridiculous but you know what, what else did I have? He was the children's father and I decided to concede to his aggressive insistence. We decided to give the marriage a second chance. We moved in together in yet another shithole on 45th Street. I knew it was never going to work between Wesley and me ever again. For my children I made the attempt. In my heart, I knew it was really over before Danni was even born. I just had nowhere to go. Sad but true.

This new place was not far enough from 53rd St. to make any impact on my recent activities, a mere few blocks away. So, needless to say, I didn't stop seeing Russell, I just adjusted my game. Russell was also content to stay in the closet and come out to play whenever I needed to play with him. This was the best situation for me. I needed a distraction to help me stomach living with Wesley. What I really wanted to do was run away screaming and never look back in the hopes that what I left behind would just disintegrate and cease to exist. Life doesn't work that way as we all know.

We moved there in September of 1996. In November of 1996, I decided I wanted another child. After Danni was born, I had two miscarriages both at twelve weeks and two years apart from each other that left a deep wound within me. I wanted to try again and I was determined at that point not to suffer another child by allowing Wesley to be its father. Adam and Danni were now 11 and 9 years old respectively. I approached my lover with the idea of becoming a donor to fulfill my need. He agreed with little coaxing. The poor kid was no match for my manipulative ways. He was mine to do with as I pleased.

I didn't hold it against him that he didn't want to marry me to help with getting my green card. First of all, it's considered illegal if it's not for love but who said we didn't love each other? We were always together any chance we got. Secondly, the penalties are severe if caught. Third, he was still young and the thought of marriage scares away most men of any age! Maybe this new endeavor would help coax him into helping me later on. Maybe. I didn't make any bets on that.

I came off the birth control pills in November 1996. December came, nothing. January came, nothing. We were having sex often but sometimes a woman's body needs to readjust from taking the pill, especially after a long time doing so. Wesley and I had not yet slept together since we'd moved into this new place and it was now 1997. Russell and I started having issues and come the week before Valentine's Day we had it out and me, being frustrated with the whole situation just decided that I couldn't care less! Whatever!

After I calmed down a week later, I called him and he invited me over to his place (in reality his mother's since he still lived at home). He was always accommodating me. Never would he say no to me....not for anything. We made love over and over again that week. You should know what came next.......yes.....by March I found out I was pregnant! I was ecstatic! So was he! This would be his first and only child till now. He was 25 and excited. The baby's due date was November 28 that year.

I obviously didn't think things through clearly. What I thought was this. I would have this child, who would look very much like my other children because its father had similar features to their father and I would just live in misery with my husband and hope for the best. I truly never wanted Russell to be a part of anything much less the child's life! I played a very stupid game that made me the loser in the end. Things didn't quite work as I had planned.

Now came the hard part; I had to sleep with my husband to validate the child's existence. It might be hard to imagine, but in all this time we never once had any sexual relations. He tried but I simply wasn't able to bring myself to do it. Now I had to. It was making me sick to think about it. It won't be an easy feat; I would need to give in at least one time to his advances and soon if my plan was to work. I eventually did.

The memory still makes me sick to my stomach to this day. Oh lawd. I felt dirty. This was a man I called husband. This was a man I had slept with for twelve years of my life. This was a man that I now despised. His rod felt the same as a tree branch might feel I thought. He stank. The smell of his semen was like none I've smelt before. How is that possible? Imagine feeling dirty while your own husband makes love to you. That's no milk and sugar. Thank goodness it was quick and the last time it ever happened. Now that I think back, how I was able to go through with it was beyond me.

As the pregnancy progressed, Russell, suddenly, wanted to be part of everything. He was so interested and wanted to know and hear everything for every step of the way. This was all new and pleasantly refreshing for me. Was I really going to have the opportunity to experience what it would be like to have a man that actually cared and wanted to cherish both me and his baby? Despite what I thought I wanted, this new situation was too much to let go. I craved to feel what it would be like to have that and I did. He was the best at being supportive, understanding and generous. I was happy.

Finally I knew what it was like for other women who had a man take care and nurture them emotionally. That was what I needed. It's what I've always needed. Money is not the way to my heart. Its emotional nurturing and soothing that will win my heart every time. He hit a home run! I was gone. No matter where we are today in our own separate lives, I will always cherish that time together especially during my pregnancy. It was a very special time in my life.

CHAPTER NINE

I worked until November 28. I was huge, my feet were swollen all the time and it was very difficult to take the subway everyday and stand on the train for whatever time the ride to and from work took. It was almost winter now and being asthmatic with the air much thinner and the added weight it was just a chore to move around.

On December 3, I began experiencing contractions. It started almost as soon as I woke that morning and continued throughout the day into night with increasing frequency and intensity. I watched Grease 2 all day long. I love that movie; Michelle Pfeiffer did an awesome job! "I wanna cooool rider, a coooooool rider…." Come 9:30pm I knew I was ready to go to the hospital. Wesley took me to Methodist Hospital on 7th Avenue in Park Slope, where my doctor was affiliated. I was in the examination room by 10:15pm. I wanted painkillers; the midwife told me it was too soon as I was only 5 centimeters dilated. By 10:30pm I was told it was too late, I was 10 centimeters dilated. I felt like killing her fat lazy ass with her legs like tree trunks!

Wesley asked me if I wanted him to stay. How ludicrous was that? Are you freaking kidding me? You weren't there for your own children and now you wanted to be there for another man's? What a jackass! Of course I told him no and sent him home to his kids. I asked the midwife to call Russell and she did. They knew him. He was always with me at the office visits. They never once saw Wesley. She asked no questions, it was none of her business. Russell arrived within 15 minutes. Incredible. He made it just in time for the move to the delivery room.

It was 10 years since my last delivery. Obviously I had forgotten the procedure. This freaking felt like the first time all over again. "PUSH!!!!" The midwife kept yelling at me. Funny, I thought I was doing that all along. I felt like I was going to push my entire insides out onto that table. What more did she want? Then she told me, "The baby's in distress." I'm asthmatic and was now having breathing difficulty of my own so what else was going to happen? The baby wasn't getting enough oxygen either! They rushed to get me on oxygen and slapped a mask on my face. I kept removing the mask; it was irritating the heck out of me! Russell was instructed to hold my head up and keep the mask held securely onto my face. Asthmatics breathe better elevated. I needed to push otherwise this could go a whole different way that nobody wanted it to.

I gave one hard, *don't care if my guts spill onto the table push* and let out a most blood curdling scream which brought everybody that was outside running to the delivery room. It's funny now but not then. Out came my baby; my little girl. I remember that she didn't make a sound. They took her quickly out of the room. She needed immediate medical attention. Apparently she wasn't breathing. What have I done? It was all a blur for me. All I know is she was brought back in a few minutes later all cleaned up and sobbing quietly. I was still being stitched up from the delivery. They placed her on my stomach and I stared lovingly at my little runt. This was the first experience of mine having the father present and part of the birth. It was wonderful. I was ecstatic! We were ecstatic.

I was home three days later. I had made the decision to have a tubal ligation performed just after the birth of my daughter as I didn't see the need to have any further pregnancies or children after this. This entailed major surgery and an abdomen cut as long as 3 inches from my navel down. I had about twelve staples in my stomach when I got home and they were to be removed the next day.

All was well at home. A new baby brings such joy and Adam and Danni were enjoying having a baby around. My appointment with the doctor was at 5PM. I wasn't feeling well but I figured that was to be expected considering all that I've been through in the past three days. I was running a slight fever. When I arrived at the doctor's he was quite happy with my condition. He removed the staples but the area around the cut was very red which can be a sign of infection. He sent me home and asked me to call him if the fever increased and anything odd happens. My vaginal stitches were in good shape.

Shortly after we returned home things all went to hell in a handbag. There was a foul odor everywhere. Everybody was trying to trace the source. It was toxic and we couldn't escape it! What on earth was that? After a thorough search, the source was not found. We thought it would eventually go away and used massive amounts of air freshener in every room to mask the scent until it went away. I began to undress. That was when the source was revealed.

When I removed my sweater and saw the condition of my under shirt I was shocked and motionless for a minute. My white undershirt was stained in the entire abdomen area with a brownish/reddish, warm viscous substance. I was the source of that foul odor! Oh my God!

Apparently, once the staples were removed, the wound opened up and let out an infection that was building in me. It was horrible. I called the doctor immediately and he asked me to clean myself up with a wet wash cloth only and come in the next day to see him. I should go to the emergency room if it kept leaking or if I developed a high fever. That didn't happen.

I was at the doctor's first thing the next morning. He said the wound was infected and required daily cleansing, except it was very deep and so a visiting nurse was setup to come to my home twice a day to clean the wound until it became stable. I would not be able to do that myself.

The wound continued to emit steady fluid. I had the best nurse ever! She was just awesome. She was always punctual, gentle and fun to have around. The kids liked her a lot too. Then one day, I felt so cold; I knew it was fever but I wasn't worried. I was wrapped up in a comforter from head to toe on the loveseat in the living room when she arrived. I heard her say to the kids, "Is that your mom under there?" They must have nodded because I didn't hear them say anything. She touched me. "Ms. Peters." Then she shook gently shook me. "Ms. Peters...." A little louder but not much. It was so cold I didn't want to open the covers at all to let the air in but she made me do it. She looked at me funny and then took my temperature which read 103. She called the doctor immediately. He told her to send me to the hospital as of pronto! I can't remember how I got to the hospital or if anyone was with me but I think I was by myself. I don't remember anyone I know being near me.

By the time I arrived at the hospital, my temperature was 104. They rushed me into emergency and my doctor was there within the next fifteen minutes. I was weak but alert. He ordered an internal MRI with contrast of my abdomen. He suspected something was very wrong. I had to drink what seemed like two gallons of toxic waste which of course was only contrast dye. It was disgusting! I thought I would hurl!

Anyways, about two hours later they took me into that room to perform the test. A small incision was made just above my navel and a long probe inserted into my abdomen. It was just me and the technician. This is all a blur for me and since there's nobody to corroborate theses facts they may not be fully correct in sequence.

I was admitted shortly thereafter and placed to lie on an electric cooling pad with bags of ice placed under my armpits and between my legs. For 24 hours they did this in an attempt to break the fever but the fever broke them and had risen to 106. They said I had a developed a cyst. Luckily for me the surgeon on call that evening in the emergency room was actually the Chief of Surgery. He was filling in for someone who wasn't able to come in for their shift. This being said, he would be the one to perform any surgeries on any patients admitted at that time if that patient required surgery. He came into my room the next day and said, "I can't wait for the fever to break, I need to operate right away."

I don't remember much after that. I do remember intense pain waking me from a deep sleep and slowly became aware of my surroundings as I awoke. I was in a regular hospital room, IV attached and in a totally weakened state. I guess the monitor that was attached to me alerted them that I had awakened. A nurse came into my room immediately to check on me. She asked me not to move around and alerted me to the fact that I had a catheter attached as well as a wide open wound in my abdomen. She took my temperature which was 103 she said. She went away after that.

The doctor came in about an hour later. He looked at me endearingly, cradled my hand in both his hands pressed to his chest and said to me, "You are a very strong woman." I looked at him questioningly. I was still groggy from the anesthesia and not fully coherent. "I needed to remove your left ovary and part of the left fallopian tube. It was encased by the infection which is why it looked to us like a cyst. We got everything. You're going to be okay now." My case surprised him he said. I should not have been able to survive such a high fever for that long without any sort of brain damage if not death. It's very unusual. What he didn't know was that fevers for me are the same as a runny nose. I had so many high fevers as a child that my body developed a tolerance for them. He didn't need to worry about me suffering any long term effects from a high fever! The effects are already there if you ask some people's opinions.

I was in the hospital for seven days! I had enough and was insistent on going home. The fever was no hindrance to me. I was in full control of my faculties by then and wanted the hell out of dodge. The next day would be Christmas Eve and I had not seen my baby and my older children for what seemed like ages! I would not spend Christmas in there if I had to walk out on my own. The doctor said to me, "I will let you leave if your fever drops to at least 100." I must have willed it to go down because by the next day it did drop to exactly 100 and I was released!

Wesley came and got me out of the hospital on December 24 around 3PM. I was dirty, smelly and in desperate need of a good shampoo! I had him take me directly to Toys R US. Now I look back and think I must be a mad woman! I had bandages on my stomach covering a wound that was still bleeding and would be for the next month or so. I could barely stand straight or walk but I would not have my kids suffer because of this. I was being punished for my deeds; they should not suffer any consequence because of it!

I was so happy to get home and take a shower, wash my hair and wear my own clothes and most of all, see my children and hold my newborn! It was a reasonably good Christmas after all. I survived my near death experience and took my punishment bravely. I knew what I had done. I was not angry but very, very repentant.

That wound remained open until late March of 1998. I went back to work in early March still with daily dressings of gauze bandaged to my stomach to absorb the fluids and protect the opening. It could not be closed. Being so deep it needed to heal well from the inside out. I have a 4 inch zigzagged scar now to remember the ordeal by. Life went on as it always will. I was on a different path now and there was no turning back.

It was soon June and my daughter was now six months old. I went to visit Russell one night. I would usually take the baby with me on the few occasions that I did this. That part of things didn't stop, if anything, I became more brazen. My marriage had never revived.

I was getting ready to leave for work around 7AM the next morning. There was a hickey on my neck, a remnant of our love making the night before and I was wearing a scarf. A scarf in the summer! Ding, ding, ding! Alarms went off for Wesley. Dunno when his eyes actually opened, but they obviously had. He brought notice to this and took the scarf off! What was revealed to him sent him off the deep end! He went ballistic! He started yelling and screaming and asking all the right questions. He made it very easy for me. Me who didn't give a rats' ass about his feelings or how he would react or what the consequences of this would mean.

This was it. After 14yrs., finally, the day had come and I was drooling with delight and strangely calm despite the volatility of the situation. It was surreal. He asked, "Is that baby even mine Deborah? "No." I looked him dead in his eyes. How much more simple could he have made it? He asked, "Is it Russell's?" I said "Yes." Jeez, life couldn't be this easy could it? No, it isn't, which I soon came to find out. This was the only easy part.

Well, life became a small whirlwind thereafter. Wesley moved out the next week and it was me and my kids against the world. Russell was always there to provide any emotional support that I needed, but that never really was supposed to be his place and it was not what I wanted, but it didn't stop me from using what was offered to me. I needed the support. This was hard and I was not prepared for it. On the one hand, I was ecstatic but on the other I was freaking scared out of my mind at what the future had in store for us!! I never even thought of Wesley after that. I looked forward to our future with wide open eyes and much anticipation.

CHAPTER TEN

The first order of things needed to be a new job. This part-time thing wasn't going to work. There was no way I could pay rent and take care of three children one being an infant on what I was making. I had to move fast. Wesley wanted to spite me and make me beg for help. I took him to court for child support instead.

I loved my job and hated the thought of leaving my friends behind but a woman has to do what she needs to, to take care of her children. The lioness must feed her cubs! Vickie was then working at an investment bank where there was an open administrative assistant position that was in the General Counsel's office. She helped get an interview setup and I went for it. Desperation would allow anybody to sell their soul. I sold my skills like I was a hooker trying to get money out of a mark. Not once did I ever allow my immigrant status to enter my mind. There was no place for trepidation here.

The job became mine but truly I was not qualified for it. By now I could talk the talk and walk the walk, so who would question me? My strategy was to 'fake it till I made it'. Its how I've approached most situations till then. However, that approach was not successful this time and the ruthlessness of corporate America soon displayed itself in one the worst imaginable ways. I experienced it firsthand!

I left my old job for my new with great excitement and anticipation. I was doing it. I was making my way independent of any man. Well, kinda - sorta. Russell was paying the daycare for his daughter so he was doing his part to help out. At least I didn't have to do that. The kids were now 10 and 12, in middle school and able to go and come on their own so I managed my household remotely. Yeah, that was the American style of family life. Direct by phone with minimal physical presence.

In my new post, I was the assistant to the assistant general counsel of this foreign-owned investment bank. I was in awe. My last company had a staff of about seventy-five with small remote locations globally. This was a huge, global organization with thousands of staff. There was a small knot of fear in my gut that never went away whilst I was there. It was hard to fake it. I didn't quite have the software experience I needed, and even though I taught myself almost everything I knew up until then, it was taking a much longer time than they were willing to tolerate.

They recognized my inexperience. Almost at the end of my three month probationary period, I was asked to leave. Reason being, it wasn't working out. Never have I been fired. I am a good worker. Diligent, smart and loyal. I remember someone from human resources calling me to come to their office. Puzzled, I went to the 3rd floor to her office. There I saw my boss and immediately knew this wasn't good. My first thought was that I screwed something up really good.

"Sit", my boss said. She never rose from her position. She was nervous, I could tell by her jittery demeanor. She was a tough one too so seeing her nervous made me even more anxious. "This isn't working out," she said. We looked right into each other's eyes. She waited for my response which never came. It had yet to dawn on me the meaning of the situation. "Deborah," The HR person chimed in. I had forgotten she was in the room. "Today will be your last day. You will be escorted to your desk to remove your personal possessions if any and then out of the building. Please surrender your ID to me now." I don't recall my boss saying anything further to me. I was stunned and did what they asked of me automated. The enormity of this reality weighed heavily on me and I broke down...even before I left the building. My professional ego was mortally wounded. It was two weeks before Christmas. This was awful and scary.

I did start a new relationship during that time with someone I met through Vickie. His name was Devon and he too was employed by the organization. He worked in accounts payable. He was very supportive and tried his best to comfort me. He was younger than me but not truly compatible. He was a liar and an impressionist, two qualities that I loathe in a human being. Obviously, he was not going to be around very long but I needed him right now.

Devon was sweet but just not the one for me. He lived with his mother and sister and was the financial head of the household. There's something to be said for a young man that unselfishly takes care of his mother, no matter how much he might complain. He helped me during the holidays to get my children some presents so as not to disappoint the poor souls. But that didn't pay the rent nor put food on the table.

I applied for unemployment benefits. This is a benefit that you receive when you get fired or laid off a job, but not when you resign unless your employer has no problem with it. It's a payment deducted from your paycheck to cover your needs should you ever lose your job. There is a maximum allowed limit though so those making high salaries will never be able to survive on what it pays. The first time you apply would take five weeks before the first check was issued. We could starve to death by then! That of course, was also when the department of labor didn't care about your immigrant status, they just needed to see that you worked and put in your time in order to qualify.

Russell too was very supportive. He works in construction and makes good money so he was my main source of food. That left the rent. The landlord had to wait. I couldn't wait for unemployment. I went back to the employment agency.

The next seven months were hellish and torturous for me. Devon, bless his foolish heart, was history by February. He would frustrate me to all limits till I just told him one day, "You know what! Lose my number!"

The agency kept me busy working odd temp assignments all over the city which allowed me to at least manage. Rent was always behind and the jackass landlord pressured me so much you would think it was more than only one month behind. I suspected that he probably wanted me to offer him sex to keep him off my back. His actions seemed to belie that meaning. He was constantly in the apartment making suggestive comments and gestures. No way! He was married, lived in the apartment upstairs with his wife and family and looked like a giant chimpanzee! No, no and freaking no!

I worked so hard to take care of my family that till today I have not yet recovered from the strain of it all. My mental state can no longer handle high stress situations and I just tend to let them go. I simply won't deal with them at all. Leave it all in God's hands I will say. That's much easier to do and has a more effective outcome than if I even tried to handle it myself anyway. So why bother?

Come July of 1999, the agency called me to ask me if I was available for permanent employment. Were they kidding? Apparently, one of the firms where I worked on assignment earlier that year had an opening and called the agency to specifically ask if I was still available for hire. Can you believe that? I couldn't! I can't describe in words the feeling that I had at that moment. It was a smorgasbord of emotions, most good and some even sad. I was elated! I regained that feeling of self worth that I had lost.

My first day of work was August 9th, 1999 as an administrative assistant for a small, global executive search firm that's headquartered in San Francisco, CA. I loved it and I was happy. The position offered more than I was offered at the bank with much less work and there were only 11 of us in the office. It was an elite profession and offered much of the finer things in life that I was not yet exposed to. One week later, on August 15th, my mother passed away.

I told Gordon, my brother who lived in Rhode Island that he needed to go home immediately and that he should be the one to represent me for my father. You see, I am the eldest of us three, then him and then Brent. He was married to an American and so he had already received his 'Green Card' and was able to travel freely. I on the other hand could go, but they sure as heck won't let me back in! I couldn't take that risk. I had too much invested here to screw it up by going back to Trinidad. So, thanks to the never ending cause of slavery, I was unable to be at my mother's funeral and be there to comfort my father and my brother in our time of grief. The role of a daughter is very important and I am the only one of my parents. It was devastating. I was crushed and felt like many a prisoner feels I imagine.

It was sometime before I was eventually able to function again but I've never gotten over the fact that I wasn't at my own mother's funeral. To this day it feels as though my family doesn't quite understand how it was that I wasn't there, but they never can unless they lived this life here in the good old USA!

Four months later my company decided to close the NY location for good. I was jobless again. They were sensitive to my situation and loved working with me, so much so that they offered me a position in the San Francisco office. Now that's bending over backwards if I ever saw it! However, there was no way I could go and so I bid them farewell in February of 2000.

Here begins a new and weird chapter in my corporate experiences in NY. One of the Managing Partners at the firm that closed interviewed at another search firm and was hired as the Chairman of the firm. He took his assistant with him and liked me so much that he arranged for me to interview with the CEO of the firm. The day I met June Gilbert was the beginning of many new life lessons for me. Harsh and horrid but many good ones too. After meeting with her for ten minutes she hired me.

I sat across from her in an office that looked like a paper recycle bin was emptied on her desk which was all wood and of Asian design. It was a magnificent piece with a high back, upholstered chair to match. There was a six foot fish tank bubbling to the right of her desk filled with various colors of gold fish. Her office was on the twentieth floor of the building and she had windows on three sides with a view of other high rises surrounding it. There was a framed piece of artwork displaying different poses of a naked man and woman, genitals exposed that I never noticed until six months after I began working there. There was a sago palm tree in a huge terra cotta pot in one corner. The woman has flair and I felt an instant connection with her.

Ms. Gilbert was in her late fifties, 5ft. and maybe 90lbs. She was overflowing with energy and her big, blue piercing eyes danced all over her face. She has a beautiful shock of short, blond highlighted hair. She wore a blue leather tight fitted pants and a leopard print tight fitted blouse with a pair of boots that were at least four inches high! She was a character and a half. The woman was intriguing to say the least and could be quite intimidating if you can be intimidated. She hired me at an even higher salary than my previous four month stint. It's just the way it's done here. You always progress in salary never regress unless there is something horribly wrong with either you or the economy. I must have been doing something right I thought; God was smiling on me if not for me for the sake of my kids. I didn't know the price I had to pay in order to earn what I did.

This was my full introduction into slavery corporate style. Up until this point I had never witnessed racism, exploitation, treachery, skullduggery, greed and envy all in one organization. Maybe it's because it's a female- owned company? I dunno.

I was plunged into the realms of the rich, filthy rich, obnoxious and rude, egotistical C-suite world of corporate America. It was swim or sink. I know how to swim so there was no way that I could sink!! I swam for my life many times. What a whirlwind of events. Eight years at June's company is enough for another story of this same length! I learned about high-end fashion and all its designers. I learned about all the fancy restaurants, wines, food and the etiquette to go along with it. I learned to talk their talk and walk their walk. I became powerful and she saw and loved it! I was her creation, her little prodigy and she enjoyed showing me off to her clients and friends. She became a surrogate mother of sorts. That relationship evolved into the strangest relationship ever.

She started to become obsessive/possessive when it came to me. She treated me like shit most of the time, and then showered me with gifts in apology. When her friends or clients made jest of stealing me away from her, she practically locked me in a closet to keep me out of sight for a while until that died down. She never wanted me to understand my importance, but I knew. Come on, I'm not stupid but that was her own underestimation and the reason for her ultimate demise. She assumed that my naiveté was stupidity; now who was the stupid one?

I quit twice and she begged, her husband begged and her partners begged me to return. She was a CEO that nobody would work with for long. Everyone ran away....literally. Her reputation in the industry was horrid. People knew of me that I never once met much less knew of because of her. I would go places and people would say to me, "So YOU'RE Debbie." I made her look good. I dealt with the clients. I kept the friends happy. I kept the house keeper happy. I kept the support staff and even some of the managerial staff happy. She caused them all pain. It worked for us. I was indispensible to her and she knew it and hoped and prayed that I didn't. I did, but I am a humble person and never abused that situation in the way a born and bred American might. It's called class and you can't buy it. It's born and bred. It probably doesn't reside in the US unless it migrated here. Sad but true. It is a classless place that thrives on its love of money.

That is the basis of life in America. It's a land built on debt. The more you have the more established and recognized you are. Isn't that a ridiculous system? It's an impressionistic society in a country that has no natural resources but manpower complete with their lies and deceit intended to blind anyone who is unfamiliar with the depth of such vile behavior.

CHAPTER ELEVEN

One day, almost three years after I started working for her, June and I were having lunch at Hema, a Japanese restaurant around the corner on 48th Street just off Madison Avenue where the office was located. She ate there every freaking day! I don't know how she did it. It was customary for her to ask me to join her at times as she felt she worked better outside of her office. Sometimes it was at the hairdresser next door or at her apartment down in the West Village. We had a good camaraderie going. I understood her and she needed me.

Out of the blue she asks, "Do you have your papers?" I was surprised and even more so by my own answer. I told her 'No' flat out. For some foolish reason I trusted her. She was so crooked it was comical. Anyways, she then proceeded to shock me further by saying that I should start the process going and she would support it. I almost fell off the stool at the bar where we sat. This crooked bitch looked like the sweetest of angels to me at that moment. I deserved an Emmy award for my performance. I said, "Ok." That was it. Then maybe "thank you" of course. Anybody who knows me would know that I'm not one for many words. Except of course when I'm pissed off then you would wonder who the heck is this she devil?

You can imagine the speed at which I got to an attorney to start the process. I was now in this country for almost sixteen years! All I could think about was going home to see my father and brother. I was excited and worked with even more fervor with the anticipation of going home very soon. Ha! Yet another delusional thought on my part.

This was going to be a long, drawn out, pretty expensive process! The years of waiting with one thing or another being requested you would think I was a mass murderer or some Taliban terrorist! The application went into the labor department in 2002 and I finally received a notice from them approving it in 2006.......can you believe that? The immigration application hadn't even been submitted yet mind you. I should tell you that during those years, Ms. Gilbert used and abused me to no end. She knew what she was doing. This was a 'chop shop' corporate style with cherries on top!

The attorney I retained had been paid $1,500 to do practically nothing. She was an all around attorney that claimed to practice all areas of law. A 'charge and bail' attorney like my beau would say. When the labor department needed anything it was a waste of time calling her. I did my own research and replied to them myself on behalf of my company of course. All the documentation came to the firm and I got them immediately rather than wait to get a copy from my attorney. That money included the immigration application which she had no part of going forward.

I had no faith in her and didn't need this messed up because of her ignorance of the law. You can find attorneys like her on any corner and they are just out to take the money of the ignorant and there are many ignorant people out here. The law is on the same level as a tongue twister in America. It could go all around and downtown. You could end up in a huge black hole if you don't know what the heck you're doing! I am a quick study. They could only get me once! I took the reins and led my own horse from here on. That scheister owes me a freaking refund!

The Immigration and Naturalization Service has an informative website complete with all you will need to do what you need done. I did thorough research and completed any and all applications, submitted them with all supporting documents requested and then sat back and waited. One and a half years later, in November 2007, I received a notice that the application for an 'alien worker' was approved and now an application to adjust my status in order get a 'green card' to travel home was the next step. This of course carried a penalty fee of $1,000USD plus the application fee of another $1,400USD for overstaying the originally allowed stay upon entry into the country of six months.

All this was coming out of my own pocket and not the company's. Ask yourself, who was really benefiting from it all? Me or Ms. Gilbert? I would love to hear all your answers. I scraped this money together somehow and submitted the application. It took them all of four months to deny it. Yeah…..deny it. Why? Why would this happen? After eight years of torture at this company, all the stress associated illnesses, failure as a mother, tension at work and the general hatred of the job, they deny me……well……..a decision needed to be made now. What should I do? I felt deflated. I didn't need to stay there anymore; there was nothing to get out of it but maybe an impending early death via a stress related heart attack or stroke. I could leave now and find a new job somewhere else less stressful. I needed to think clearly.

A few years before, my son Adam started getting into all sorts of things boys do and not the good things. Absent father and remote mother is not a good equation for stable kids. Boys need more hand holding than girls, although I'm sure some of you will beg to differ! Mine was no exception. He was also a momma's boy.

I was doing the best I could on the monies I earned. I was not able to provide my teenagers with the vast wardrobe of brand name clothing that some of their friends were tailored in. Peer pressure must have been an issue for my son. Girls can get away with wearing any ensemble. As long as it accentuated their assets who cared how much it cost! The clothes make the man and my son needed to look the part of his friends. His friends however, were fitting in by stealing the clothes and shoes they wanted from the local department stores. They were petty thieves and had a new recruit.

The stealing began. Along with the stealing came the never ending lies and cutting of school. He brought his cohorts into the home when I left for work. He did this for months unbeknownst to my ignorant self. Those he brought into the home stole his baby sister's milk and sold it. I got her milk from WIC, a government subsidized program to assist qualified mothers of babies. I qualified because I couldn't afford the three plus dollars for a can of baby formula on my salary!

Things were rapidly changing for the worse with the boy. I was at my wits end trying to figure out what the heck to do. Neither my brothers nor any of my relatives as far as I can recall were ever like this. Of course, his father and his side of the family were! We were like night and day his father and I. Take some advice girls, research his family and background before you say 'I do" or venture to have children with him. Genetics account for many an armed robber, murderer or serial rapist! Nobody ever told me that and look at what happens years later. All I heard from my parents was "do as I say and don't ask any stupid questions!' I always needed an explanation; otherwise I will NOT do as you say! My own stupidity is what got me here anyways, so I'm trying to help some of you who as yet might not know or it might not be too late for you!

As they say in my country – goat doh mek sheep – you figure it out. His behavior was incomprehensible to me. Whatever strategy I tried failed. I had no choice. I needed to send him to Trinidad to save him. If he stayed he would end up dead or in prison. The freaking irony of the whole situation is incredible. I left Trinidad for him. I wanted to provide him the opportunities that we never had in a land where the opportunities seemed endless, and where was he going – right back from whence he came, fifteen years later! Was it all for naught?? Where were the sweet beds of roses and bottles of wine they promise? Seriously. My mind was reeling. I laid it out for him just like that and gave him the choice. He chose to go back to Trinidad. What he didn't know was that he was going whether he chose that option or not, but I wanted it to be his own decision. He would need to live with his decisions. It was his first lesson in manhood. Probably his only lesson thus far.

Things get a little fuzzy here as you should understand. I was sending my only son away from me after 15 years, with no hope of ever seeing him again for who knows how long. I was disenchanted by the country and depressed amongst many other things. The pain was too much to bear but I bore it as only a woman could. I don't think there is a man alive that can sustain what a woman can. I could be wrong of course; only time will tell. My heart was heavy, literally heavy. I've heard people say that and even read it but never felt it until then. It really can feel heavy. Like a brick in your chest just weighing in there ready to fall to the bottom of your stomach if it could and eventually kill you. I watched my little boy go through the security gates at JFK on his way to his own new adventures in life….without me.

I am happy to say I did not cry, well, not for him to see anyways. When he was out of sight and I turned around to leave the airport was when it all began to flow from me. It was then that I remembered that I wasn't alone. I hadn't realized that there was no external sound around me all this time. It was as though Adam and I were in a void where no one and nothing else existed but the place we were in. I believe I had held my breath all this while. Slowly I started hearing the familiar noises of voices and luggage wheels rolling along the floors. It yanked me back into reality. I became aware of Russell, Danni and Raven walking alongside and looking at me mumbling to each other. I remember one of them saying, "Is she crying? She's crying…" Yes I was, not hysterically, but steadily. It's a good thing Russell drove us there because I would never have been able to take us home. The tears couldn't stop its incessant flow and my body trembled uncontrollably. I was a total mess. I think I was the only one who really understood the enormity of the situation and what it meant. It was better that way. Let me bear it for us all. My back is broad.

Now it was just me and the girls, a 13 year old and a 3 year old. I felt unsafe for some strange reason. The comfort of having a son around was gone. Vulnerability set in big time! This is not a safe place to live. The predators come in all shapes, sizes and guises. You can't trust anyone. How was I supposed to continue to be a remote mother with only girls at home? They need protection. We need protection. I leaned on Russell more than ever. He and his friends needed a place to hang out and smoke their weed away from the eyes of the law and I needed to show whoever was watching that we were not going to be easy prey. There would be at least five grown men to get past before you can get to any of us! It was not the best of situations but it was all I had at the time. There was no family any place close by. They were it. So we formed a sort of dysfunctional, adoptive family and bonded.

Raven had many uncles, Danni many a big brother and I had many, young, male friends. You can imagine I was the talk of the area! People can be so ignorant and judgmental when they have nothing else to talk about, and they talked, and talked and talked. I'm sure I haven't even heard half of what was said but what I did hear was so distasteful that I really didn't need to hear anymore. They could all go to hell! None of them fed me, paid my bills or housed me! What they thought meant naught to me and very soon, none of them even existed in my world, the one that I had created for myself and my family. We were ok for the time being. This all happened in early 2001; the same year the world trade center was demolished by unknown perpetrators.

CHAPTER TWELVE

Life took on a whole new outlook. I began managing Adam in Trinidad remotely from New York and was still able to do so here with Russell's help. See, he is in construction so he gets home from work by 2:30pm for the latest. I didn't get home from work until almost 7PM. As they say, one hand washes the other. He would get to my place by 5:30pm or 6; that would mean that Danni would be home alone only from 3:30pm to when he got there. That worked for me as he would also pick Raven up from the daycare so that all I needed to do was come directly home. The babysitter was on the same block so it was not too much of a hassle for him and he enjoyed doing it anyways. He was the proud new father. It was pleasing to see. I never had that with my ex-husband, Wesley. He was never proud or grateful or anything good. He was just selfish and it was always all about him and everyone else should follow or be left behind. What an awful life that was. Why would I have thought at that time that Russell would turn into the jerk he eventually did? Maybe it's just a common denominator in men, I dunno.

So, it was just me, the girls and the …………guys? Yup. A whole bunch of them. As the years progressed, it was evident that there was never going to be anything that will develop between Russell and me more than what already existed. We were special friends with fringe benefits. We all know what that means. Everyone has one or two or many of those. I was not yet ready for any serious relationship anyway. I wanted to enjoy a bit of freedom which I never really had. I went from my father's house to a marriage of disgust and now to freedom! I was gonna do what I wanted, when I wanted, how I wanted and with whomever I wanted …..and that is exactly what I did!

When Raven was two I met an African named Gerard. He was a cab driver here in Brooklyn and also an accomplished musician in his native land. He too was another victim of 'the dream'. He is not well educated, but has a good, honest nature. He was very patient most of the time but I could try the patience of a saint so of course, an inevitable end was in our future!

Gerard was six feet tall, bald headed, light brown and built like a stallion. There was no difference between the way his ass looked and that of a stallion. I think there might not have been much difference between the better part of him and that of a stallion as well if you get what I'm trying to say. Gerard was a sex machine. His dick worked on cue. I always felt that there was a switch somewhere that only he knew where it was. Ladies, I never thought that a woman could be oversexed but we can be. His style was so primitive! Once I got to his place I needed to strip naked and remain that way until I left. Then we had sex over and over and over and over again for hours. He did make sure I ate in between episodes though! Real caveman style! It was an incredible experience but quite draining especially with a high demand job as well.

Things were going well for a while. I was still sure that I was not yet ready for a serious relationship. It began to seem like I was heading into one with someone who worked too many hours and had very little time for me. This scenario left me up to my feminine wiles. I strayed many times. Not for lack of sex but for lack of attention and intimacy. He didn't have enough time to spend with me. I worked days he worked nights; he worked seven days a week.

After four years of nothing but lots of amazing sex and daily recounts of what was happening in the news. I told him one evening in two sentences, "This is not working for me. We need to go our separate ways." Simple as that. He understood. He had known for some time that I was not happy with the situation and he also knew I was way out of his league. I guess he too was deluding himself all along. It may have been a relationship of convenience. However, we were always honest with each other and have remained very close friends till today.

During those four years with Gerard, I met another African named Edward at a restaurant we frequented. He eventually became one of my friends with benefits. Edward had a well defined slim body, low cut hair and was at least two inches shorter than me. However, the size of his dick made up for his lack in height. If that was taken into account he could easily be six feet tall! I've never before seen anything that huge with my own eyes. The fact that he also knew how to use his tool well was a plus for us both. He was a very good lover. There was nothing he wouldn't do to please me sexually. I enjoyed him extensively.

We played here and there whenever he was around. He was from out of town and came to NY once or twice in a month to visit his then infant daughter. He and the child's mother did not have any relationship except for the connection of the child. He always insisted on us getting together when next he was around. Sure, why not? I had nothing else going on and he was fun.

Edward worked with the Department of Social Services in Virginia; at least he had escaped the rigors of hardship we were experiencing as fellow immigrants. His situation was different though. He had sisters that lived in the USA for many years that sponsored him and their parents many years before then, so he was all set to do whatever he pleased. Lucky devil.

Eventually, after a few years of knowing each other and after my relationship with Gerard ended, we made an attempt at getting together as a couple. He owned his own home in Virginia and kept insisting that we get married and live there together. It was a beautiful house too. I enjoyed the location and layout. It was an end unit, two stories with a huge garden, a garage and most importantly, lots and lots of light from all the glass doors and skylight. There was also a huge fireplace in the living room. It was a very inviting offer but I was not attracted to him in that way and could not see myself being good to him for very long. He smoked and drank too much and was a little slow upstairs if you know what I mean. Not the brightest bulb. It would not have lasted. One good thing gained from bad experiences, you learn to recognize the signs from the onset. My alarms were already sounding!

We tried the relationship thing for about five months and I decided it was not for me. You might say this was another chance to get my green card but it would have cost me too much to marry him just for that purpose. It would mean packing up my family and moving to a state where I knew no one else. The price was too high. I had begun to set limitations for myself by then. I was hardened to the situation and prepared never to leave this country except in a body bag. Then, I met a man who was so different than any I've met before. I was soon hooked and didn't yet realize it.

There I was, one day in November, 2005, sick with fever, pale and weak. By afternoon, I decided to venture out to get something to eat for the first time that day to the New Combination, African restaurant on Utica Avenue. I found that when I ate this dish called egusi soup, it usually made me feel so much better. It was a dish prepared with either bitter leaves (native to Africa) or spinach and ground egusi seeds.

I was there for not more than five minutes when he walked in. He was approximately 5' 7", muscular build, nice dark skin, almost white teeth……….no, I was not buying a horse………and wearing the most outrageously designed body hugging shirt ever! No exaggeration; it was wild! There was also an old man's hat on his clean, shiny bald head. He was dark chocolate if I ever saw it. I prefer milk chocolate but I'm always willing to be swayed by the right morsel of another flavor. They do say dark chocolate is a very good antioxidant.

I was sitting on a stool right at the counter, too weak to stand for a long time. They knew me well there; I was a regular patron for many years. The manager was always trying to get my number and would never stop trying even though he knew it was futile. I was placing my order when he arrived and he stood diagonally to my right just behind me. When I placed my order I looked back at him so he would know I was done and he should proceed. He had a smirk on his face and his eyes were lit up. He was obviously amused. I knew what was next. It would not have been the first nor be the last time someone would question me about my knowledge of African cuisine. He is African too. I suppose he is who I was being groomed for with my previous relationships. Maybe?

So, then came the line I was expecting and there went the usual response which sparked more conversation. "You know what egusi is?" "Yes I know what egusi is. I like egusi." His voice was like chocolate syrup flowing over vanilla ice cream if you can understand that analogy. I wanted to hear more of it!

He was beguiling and intriguing and we developed a wonderful dialogue filled with quips and puns until we came to a point where he bragged about losing one of his jobs because he beat up his boss. He was even laughing when he said it. I was appalled and disgusted. What kind of miniscule mind would find that amusing? I practically asked him such but in a much nicer way. "You think that's funny?" I asked as I looked at him. I'll tell you this, he can sure ride!! He back pedaled so fast that he actually got out of that smoothly!! As a matter of fact, he can still do that today. I gotta think more on this situation me thinks. Hmmmmmm.

For some strange reason, his food arrived before mine did. He handed his money to the manager who begrudgingly took it looking at the bills as though he would rather not touch them. "I'll be waiting outside for you when you come out." I said ok but wasn't really interested. I didn't even turn around to watch him leave. I had a boyfriend already and a boy toy in Russell; I didn't need anything more than that at the moment. I kinda wondered why he wasn't scared at the sight of me since I looked like death warmed over but go figure. Men can be strange creatures at times. So he went out and I turned my attentions to whatever was going on around me and forgot all about him.

It was then that I noticed the manager's expression. He was evidently not happy about the entire exchange that he just witnessed. He didn't say anything about it though. He opened the freezer that was behind him and offered me a Guinness stout to drink while I waited for my food, which was taking quite a suspiciously long time to come out from the kitchen I must say! I was probably in there for another fifteen minutes since my Adonis left me in wait or vice versus I believe. The delay seemed deliberate but we will never know for sure.

Once my food was in hand I proceeded out of the restaurant to my car which was parked immediately in front. Honestly, I don't know if it was because I was sick but I had totally forgotten about him until I heard someone blowing their car horn repeatedly. I looked around just in time to see him emerge from his own vehicle a few car lengths back. I was surprised and smiled at his diligence. "I can't believe you waited." He asked for my number; I gave it to him. I told him I had a boyfriend and he said we could just be friends. No harm I thought. He proceeded to dial the number immediately which also surprised me. I had to ask, "Did you think I gave you a false number?" At the same time my cell phone was ringing. It was him of course. We joked about his act and both got into our respective cars. It was November in NYC. It was too freaking cold to be standing in the streets talking! He kept me on the line and we continued talking on our way to our respective destinations. I truly enjoyed our conversation, more so because he said there were no strings attached. That I didn't realize at the time, was also what the spider said to the fly! His name is Lionel.

We've been together ever since. By mid December he gave me an ultimatum, "decide who you want to be with, me or that guy in Virginia". We had just started sleeping together. It was an experience like no other. I was carried away by the intensity and abounding passion that was brewing between us. He worked some magic on me I'm sure of it! Hey, I knew that other was not going anywhere and I didn't know where this might lead but the prospect of hope is a better route than that of doom isn't it? I chose the blue pill. I have never regretted that choice to this day. This was no laborer or son of a laborer. This was the son of a Harvard graduate and professor. This was the brother of doctors and lawyers. This was a professional himself with an enigmatic brain. This was the challenge I needed in a man!

Needless to say, I needed to end things with my present boyfriend, Edward who had no idea things were on its last ebb. How was I going to do this without incident? Since he lived out of town, I had no choice but to call and lay it down easy. Edward claimed surprise, I don't know why, and tried to talk me out of my decision. That was a futile effort! Everybody knows when a woman's mind is made up there's nothing anyone can do to change it. He was history and he needed to know that. I already did. He eventually ceased arguing with me over it and feigned acceptance. I should have known he would not have given up so easily.

Christmas Eve came, the kids were at their respective father's and I was home alone. Lionel went to Rhode Island to deal with his own mess that would also be another dialogue worthy of a few hundred pages in itself! We had been getting to know each other better day by day. We were enjoying this budding friendship. Edward kept calling and calling that night and I refused to answer the phone. I knew what it meant you see. He was in town and wanted to see me. It was late, around 11:30pm or thereabouts. He usually drove up from Virginia around that time so I was not suspect of anything out of the norm.

He showed up at my apartment and began banging on the door. What the heck? I had no choice but to let him in to avoid the scene that was ensuing. He would wake the neighbors and I didn't need that.

I was really irritated by all the calls and now the attempt at a public display. I was ready to kill him and he didn't know it. Little did I know that it was close to me being killed should have been my premonition.

He immediately had his hands and lips all over me, groping, kissing, and fondling me as I opened the front door. I kept retreating with each advance till I found myself back against the wall just outside my bathroom. Now he pressed himself firmly against my body's full length and was kissing and biting my lips and pulling my underwear down from my waist whilst he placed his hands between my legs. In my attempt to push him off, I teetered on my own legs that were now strapped closed around my ankles by my underwear and fell forward....... toward the corner of the marble table that was directly in front of me! Had I not put my hands forward to brace my fall, my head would have hit the tables' edge and that probably would have been the last night I breathed the toxic air of that apartment.

I flew into a venomous rage! I hurled curse words at him while pulling my panties up from around my ankles and practically chased him out of my apartment. I wanted to finish him. He used his better judgment and left immediately out of the same door he entered which had remained open because of his sudden onslaught of perverted advances.

I sat on the sofa holding my face in the palms of my hands and shaking at the implications of the whole scenario. Would he have left me there hurt or would he have taken initiative? I believe he would have run like the pussy I know him to be and my children would be motherless today. I was angry at myself for being constantly involved with the wrong people. I needed to do a serious self analysis and make some firm decisions as to where my life was headed and how to change direction quickly. At that moment, I wished Lionel was there with me.

CHAPTER THIRTEEN

The following years were a series of ups and many downs with Lionel. We saw each other every day since we met and spent every night together. Finally, in October 2007, we decided it really made no sense maintaining two apartments and he gave his up and temporarily moved into mine. He's in real estate so he would be able to find us something more suitable soon. Besides, my place was cheaper and with the kids, it made more sense to just do it that way. Except, with a male ego the size of Tanzania that became truly difficult if not downright psychotic!

The African culture is quite different from that of the western world. It is a chauvinistic, egotistical and submissive culture depending on your gender. I'm sure you can guess which gender submissive was attached to. That is definitely not the case in this part of the world and where am I from? Exactly. My own culture dictates equality of responsibilities within the home except for the obvious needs of brawn versus comfort and nurturing.

Lionel was also a victim of the dream. His trials had been severe and when we met he could be compared to a wounded animal still licking his wounds. I wonder today had I known it all before hand if I would have still taken the blue pill? So, I had a man with an illness that required daily medication, severe emotional trauma and in the same immigrant predicament as mine. Sounds like a recipe for disaster yes? It was, for quite some time.

We disagreed on almost everything. The ways of his world did not work here and I was constantly trying to make him understand that which appeared to be just nonsense in his eyes. He would never get it. He is an exceptional being with an equivalent mind. It would take a woman of similar character and intellect to compliment him. I believe I am that woman.

There's one thing that I would like to share that truly boggles the mind. New York City is a city filled with immigrants of various legal status yet those that abuse immigrants of such status are actually those that were in the same or similar situation at one time or another in their own lives. It is amazing and saddening. I've heard it called the Ph.D. syndrome – pull him down syndrome. It's a deadly, man-made affliction and prevalent amongst the black community more than any other. Lionel was smack in the middle of such a situation. It took much coaxing and support to make him trust in himself and make the decisions that would allow him to think outside of the box that was given him to succeed. Fortunately, I was able to encourage him along such paths and he has since soared to higher plains. I am so very proud to see him succeed despite all the inhibitions we both faced as a result of our immigrant status.

We were now two years into our relationship and a lengthy time of turbulence between us. During this time, my older daughter Danni decided she could not accept my new relationship and moved in with her father. It broke my heart. She was very special to me for many reasons as you've seen earlier in this missive. She was my right hand and she was gone. She did not look back. I never thought that at nineteen a child would still have the delusion that her parents could reunite even after ten years of separation. That just seems incredulous to me. Life went on. It was very difficult for Raven who was now nine years of age to deal with her sister's departure, but I teach my children to take life in stride and make the best of it and I lead by example, so just follow the leader.

During this time as well, my landlord decided he didn't quite like the fact that I now had a live-in boyfriend and embarked on a quest to destroy any small comfort of a home that we made in his decrepit, illegal basement apartment. He and Lionel got into it on many occasions and my boy enjoyed taunting that stupid man. He giggled gleefully after any incident with the landlord or his even more stupid wife who by the way could be mistaken for a man unless you looked closely. No wonder he wanted a piece of me. Imagine sleeping next to that every night. Huh!

By August 2008, we were moving on up, not to a deluxe apartment in the sky but to a beautiful apartment in Sheepshead Bay which is one of the finer areas of Brooklyn because ....it's where many of the whites lived. Sad but true. The house was situated on a quiet street with no parking rules. I never knew such places existed. What a refreshing thing to not have to scramble and move your car from side to side for street cleaning rules every day except for Wednesday depending on where you were exactly. The quiet seemed deafening at first. Nothing but birds chirping on mornings and the wind howling through the alley ways. I had not realized how accustomed I was to the sound of sirens and gun shots. The human mind is so adaptable and truly amazing. Oh, and we were the only black people on the block. I hated it!

If you wonder why I hated it let me tell you. Most of the residents in the areas were much older, whites that have lived there for many years and owned the homes they lived in. They considered the area their own and now blacks were infringing on their space. There's nothing anyone can say to dispute that fact. I felt it every second of every day I lived there. It radiated from their eyes when they looked at you and from their breath when they made their lame attempts at conversing with you. I loathe hypocrites! I don't know if Lionel ever saw it but he did try to penetrate their shields with his charisma. I couldn't care less and never once tried.

This is when I made one of the boldest moves of my life. I decided to quit my job at that zoo to pursue other options. This was June 2008. I was confident that I would find another job easily. I did not take into consideration the economic downturn and increased rate of unemployment. I felt I could get unemployment benefits for a while and that would alleviate some of the financial stress until I landed the right job. Of course, I was basing this assumption on my last experience with unemployment. I hadn't realized things had changed and changed drastically!

I applied and was denied due to my then immigrant status. I was considered an illegal immigrant since my immigrant application was not approved and I didn't have work authorization. These times are now post 9/11 and way of life in the USA had changed drastically. Many more stringent immigrant rules had been implemented. I had been working for the past twenty two years and now was not able to enjoy the benefits of my own hard labor. This is how they exploit immigrants who try to do things the right way. So now I was screwed royally. My plans all went awry. I needed some source of income and I needed it fast. It was the summer and anybody that knows anything about the economic market knows it slows to a snail's pace during the summer period. There was no way Lionel would be able to do it alone; he now worked for himself and had his own clients. But the market is the market and he needed help; what little I could provide would be better than none!

I decided to go back to the agency that was my savior some eighteen years ago and they did not let me down. Over the years I was very good to them. In my managerial roles I awarded them contracts when the needs arose. I firmly believe that one hand washes the other and I was loyal to them for life! It was very surprising to learn that the person I had dealt with all those years ago was still there except she was now a vice president. She was also a good friend and I was able to bypass all legal requirements and tests due to this long standing relationship. Imagine if I had to provide the work authorization, I would probably be homeless today and my life in ruins.

I think I received an assignment within the next two weeks that was long term which is exactly what was needed. It was a reasonable salary and it was better than nothing! This was now October and so I was pretty much penniless since June and I guess I didn't look quite as appealing to Lionel as I once did. I can attribute this assessment to his behavior toward me. It's an assumption but I feel one that's dead on.

My pride was wounded by the awful things he would say and do. I needed to keep my head up for my daughter's sake if nothing else. Again I found myself in a situation where a man felt he should step on me because I had no money of my own. Seems men value women for their monetary worth these days and not for the emotional support that they still obviously do need and get. A woman is a man's foundation and back bone. She can make or break him whether she has a penny or a million dollars! He wanted to demoralize me I was sure of it! Thank goodness for my many years of service in the armies of Wesley and June Gilbert! It would take a helluva lot to break this old horse.

Sometimes I feigned defeat to make peace. Many times it was futile to argue as I may as well have been talking to a rock. He never listened and his word was law, unrealistic as it was at times. On the many occasions when he finally understood my logic he never gave credit where credit was due. It was all of a sudden his own brilliant conclusion. What a character; sometimes it was extremely disgusting but eventually I accepted that his ego was the blinding force between us and last time I checked, I didn't have a counterforce to break that barrier. I too was learning his nature as he was mine. This class was tough man!

Anyway, my job was going well but I looked forward to making it fulltime. It was the only way that I could receive health benefits and more money. After six months they offered me the position. I was ecstatic! My boss jumped through hoops with Human Resources to get the offer finalized quickly. They bent over backwards for her. I did the criminal background check which came back all clear. I guess they never did find that body in the river......just joking! I signed the offer letter and the next Monday was my first official day as an employee. I was so happy. I loved my co-workers and they loved me! It was a wonderful environment and I could learn so much and progress quickly. Then I got the call from Human Resources.

The organization is a non-profit business and new immigration laws dictated that they participate in something called e-verify which verified whether or not a new employee is legally allowed to work in the United States. This was the first time they needed to participate. Just my freaking luck. Mine could not be verified. I had ten days to provide whatever I had to show work authorization or my employment would be terminated. I was devastated. There was no way I could do that and so after all my hard work had to leave just two weeks after my official start date. My boss could not even look me in the eye and avoided me on my last day. She was crushed and felt that I was not honest with her. She lost many nights sleep working on a plan to get me on board. How was I supposed to tell her the situation? The route I took was the better one. It could go either way and unfortunately it went the other way.

The organization felt my pain and agreed not to inform the agency of why they needed to retract my offer for employment. This was April, 2008.

So, we lived in Sheepshead Bay for eighteen months before we were asked to leave by our landlord. He was a fat, horrible sloth with self confidence issues. He was intimidated by Lionel who is his exact opposite and perhaps someone he wished he could be at least once in his miserable lifetime. I welcomed the drama. It proved a good distraction for Lionel; it distracted him from me. During the time we lived there, I spoke only to the woman that lived next door and simply because she always seemed to be outdoors whenever I was. We must have had similar schedules.

There was another more critical reason I welcomed the change; in the eighteen months there, it never once felt like a home. How could it be a home when you were not allowed to add to the interior design because your suggestions were either vetoed or needed approval before implementation? How could it when the one time you take yourself out at night found yourself locked out of your own home at the whim of the one you love? How could it when you go visit a friend who haven't seen for ten years for just two hours and find yourself locked out again at this same person's whim? Not to mention the acts of physical abuse – being physically pushed around, choked, thrown off the bed and locked out of your own bedroom. This was no home. I was a woman who took care of herself and her own for the past ten years without a man and to come to this?

Cultural differences can be detrimental to many relationships, however, I knew who I had in him and would not let his frustrations with trying to manage a western woman destroy a good thing. Of course, had he spent less time frolicking with other females out there and actually devoted more time to what was important to him a lot of what happened would not have. He was constantly making the same mistakes with women. He was a loose dog with no leash. This behavior was unbearable and I wondered how long I would be able to handle it. I could have run but I stayed. Paul paid for all and Paul was me. He should eventually understand that I am not here to hurt him; I would make him understand while I hope that he doesn't kill me first! His wounds are deep and need to heal from the inside out and I understand it would take a long time. I can wait, all I have is time. Plus, I love him and trusted in God to guide us through these early times. God has never let me down and he didn't then.

My first daughter, Danni was turning 21 in May and my immigration application would be able to go in as a petition for an alien relative. Yeah, I made her 21 years ago and raised her all on my own and she now needs to acknowledge her own mother as an 'alien relative'. Demeaning and demoralizing don't you agree? Despite it all, I had no option but to proceed with the process no matter how it bruised my pride and self respect. The application was prepared and sent in to the corresponding immigration office the day after May 21, one day after her birthday. By now I was a professional at preparing such applications and correspondence of the same nature. I needed no attorney to do this for me. Unfortunately for many, there are 'attorneys' out there that know less than they do who will take their money, intentionally prolonging the process so as to exploit the immigrant into paying and paying and paying. To swim with sharks you need to eat what they eat; to survive with sharks you need to keep them hungry. I chose to starve those bastards!

Anyway, I went back to the agency the week after I was let go, but things had slowed down. I told them the organization had experienced some immediate budget cuts and of course the last man in would be the first man out. It was an unfortunate but believable scenario knowing the economic situation at hand. They asked no further questions and agreed to find me another position.

I was again penniless and nothing came my way until July. By July however, I had received approval of my immigration application and had the work authorization in hand ready for any instance of use. I was again placed at a position in early July. I was the Executive Assistant to the Director of a combination of health sciences libraries. After six months at this position I was offered the job and again my then boss jumped through hoops to get me the hired at the highest salary she could for the position. Despite all the hurdles in her way strewn by my immediate supervisor she made it happen. My supervisor had been there for eight years and wanted to bring me in at a lower level. My boss knew my worth and bypassed her. Human Resources approved her request for a salary that was $10K more than was I was offered by the other firm just six months ago. Who gets an increase of $10K in six months? God is a good God I will always say.

My Green Card actually came in the mail on August 31. I felt nothing when I opened the envelope. I felt cheated and angry when I held it in my hands. Lionel was more excited for me than I was. After what I'd been through to get this thing, was it really worth it? I still say no till today.

My official start date as an employee of the medical center was December 14, 2009. I provided the necessary documents needed to be hired, inclusive of the green card. I've rested my weary bones there since then. 2010 started off the right way! My pride restored, Lionel's violent and hostile actions receded. Maybe it was all in my head or my own low self esteem that contributed to our troubles. It couldn't be coincidental. I had my own money now and he didn't have to bear the entire load. His ego was bigger than his wallet and pockets which led to irrational thinking and behavior at times. This is his first really *committed* relationship and he was still learning the rules. I had a much better idea than him and so had the advantage which, when I think about it could even be considered a disadvantage. Ignorance is bliss. I was not quite as ignorant.

FINAL CHAPTER

This is it. My husband, yes, that same man I've complained about far too many times has allowed me the privilege of seeing my dad and my son after all these eons of hardships. That same unselfish (at times) man, I wouldn't let him hear me say that though, that has brought me out of my miserable, dark hole back into the light of day and spiritual happiness. The moment I showed him the "Green Card" when it arrived the very first thing he said was; "Well now you should go visit your father." I was shocked.

Things had been rocky for too long with all the women and suspicious behavior. I can admit forcefully, I didn't trust him! It's so hard to trust when trust has been betrayed. It's logical to become wary of someone who has been deceptive, what's to stop them from doing it again and again? I remember thinking, 'What was he up to now?' I played along to see how far it would go.

It went so far that he purchased my ticket and even provided me spending monies even though things were a little tough at the time. I was on my way home………..even now it rings awkward in my ears. I never thought this day would come, not in a million years! I thought I would just die here in America and never see my family ever again. God is good, always good.

When one puts their trust in God it always seems to make things better. Even that trust was gone from me for some time. I remember when I used to pray every day for deliverance from this slavery. God was always in my thoughts, actions and deeds. Then I don't know what happened. I strayed. For convenience I believe and perhaps disenchantment. I was involved in too many unmentionable deeds that were so far away from what God wanted for me that I couldn't look that way. Didn't want to look that way. Just gave up and headed gleefully downhill at record speed!

That was a very dark time in my life. I was having fun or what I thought was fun. Living recklessly and daringly, but we're now past that episode. I think I can say that I am happy. Honestly happy. I have a home, a family and everything appears to be on track. A somewhat rickety track but at least not a broken track.

I wanted my first trip home to be a surprise for my family. After twenty two years why the heck not? I had to plan this well. My family already knew that the immigration application was approved and that I was just waiting to receive the Green Card. However, they did not know that I had it! My flight to Trinidad was booked for October 7 leaving JFK at 1:15am.

On that eventful morning, after the flight arrived at Piarco International Airport, I was out of customs by 6:40am. A friend of mine arranged for one of his friends to meet me and he was there waiting for me as scheduled. He is an active, Special Forces guy, trained in Brazil and the US and was even part of the squad that was assigned to President Obama when he visited Trinidad this year. T&T had been experiencing high crime rates, involving kidnapping of tourists and anyone who might look worthy of robbing. I didn't need to end up a victim of circumstance in the bushes of Lopinot or Caura!

His name is Marc Anthony. I dialed his cell phone as soon as I stepped out of customs. He answered and while on the phone we located each other. He came up to me, shook my hand and introduced himself. "Hi Debbie, I'm Marc." "Hi. Thanks so much for picking me up. I really appreciate this very much." He grabbed my bag and we headed outside.

"Oh, dat's no problem man. No inconvenience at all." He is tall, handsome, like Keanu Reeves handsome and very polite. It felt good to be amongst my people again. We left the airport driving on roads that were very unfamiliar to me now. I was thinking that I was in the same airport I left from in 1987. I couldn't be more wrong. Granted, it looked different but not so much that it couldn't just be accounted for renovation. Marc was amused at my confusion. "When was the last time you was here?" "Twenty three years ago when I left."I responded. "You think dis is de same airport you left from eh? Look over there." He pointed in the distance to an old, dilapidated building, much smaller than the one we just left. As soon as I saw it I recognized it. Marc chuckled at my expression. My head quickly became a lighthouse with my eyes as its globe, searching as far as I could see for anything and everything.

The roads were different and there were many more billboards than I could remember. The bushes on the way out remained the same though as I recognized them from the time I needed to pee really bad when I was pregnant with Adam and had no choice but to get out and water the bushes. Ha! That was something!

Even though I was amazed and captured by all that I saw, sightseeing was for later, right now I needed to call the old man and set my plan in motion. Marc allowed me to use his phone blocking his number for anonymity and I dialed my home number while he drove. My father's new wife answered. "Hello, good morning." "Good morning Betty, daddy up yet?" It was just close to 7:30am. "Debbie? No, he still sleepin." I told her that I would call back in a few minutes. In a few minutes we got to the street I lived on for the better part of my life and guess what...I passed the house straight! We had to go around the block which allowed me time to decipher which was the house. Marc parked his car a few houses away and we got out. I got the camcorder ready and he agreed to help me record this big moment.

I was so excited. He then redialed my home and my dad answered. He quickly gave me the phone. I heard my dad say, "Hello." "Hello dad. 'Mornin." "Mornin dahlin. How yuh going? Wah happen?" "Nuttin happen. Come outside nah?" Yeah…. here we go now. "Wah yuh mean come outside?" The old man was totally confused. He did sound as though he was getting up, from his bed probably and moving, heading outside as if being ordered to do so even though his logical mind was asking him why he was doing that.

See, I called him from my home in Brooklyn just last night to chat so he wouldn't even think I could be there! As we walked toward the house who do I see in the front but my bald headed brother, Brent. He lives at home with his family too. It's a pretty big house so it can accommodate a huge family like in that miniseries Dallas?

Brent looked at me stunned, got up and ran toward me with all his sweaty might and practically suffocated me with his mass drenching me in his sweat all at the same time. He can sure multi task! While I was talking with Brent, camera still going, my dad opened his front door………and just froze! We all watched as he stood there immobilized for a count of at least sixty seconds, mouth open and hands dropped to his side. He was shirtless wearing only a pajama bottom. When he could finally say something he said, "Wah yuh doing here? I didn't jes talk to you last night?" He then swaggered toward me and embraced me for quite some time in sheer disbelief.

I think he didn't quite believe his eyes or touch. At least he didn't drop of a heart attack which was my biggest fear!!! I gestured to Marc to stop recording and introduced him to everyone. I turned to him and said, "Marc, thanks again for everything." He handed me the camcorder, "It was my pleasure." He turned and left. I never saw him again.

Everyone at home was now awake. News of my arrival had spread. The rest of the morning was filled with lots of conversation and fun.

Next was my son. He lived on his own in Tunapuna, which is the next town over where I was born and only a couple of miles away. Even though I wanted to be prepared and have the upper hand when I saw him, thanks to my big mouthed brother that turned out to be impossible. He couldn't wait to call and let Adam know that I was there. I didn't find out that he had done this until Adam's surprise appearance at the house. I returned from a short trip out with my dad the same day I arrived. We went to a furniture store in Tunapuna to purchase a fold up bed. Since my arrival was a surprise, a bed was not readily available for me.

We got back to the house and Betty stepped out of the car to open the gate. She quickly ducked down and whispered to me sitting in the back, "Don't look now but Adam here." I was taken aback but quickly composed myself and jumped out of the car. About a year before, he and I had a misunderstanding I would call it and became estranged.

I locked eyes with him as he sat motionless on the porch. He had a hostile glare. We remained eyes locked until I was directly in front of him. I said to him, "what, you can't give your mother a hug? You haven't seen me for so long....." He stood up and we shared a tender, heavy, emotion filled embrace. It was sweet.

A quick, heated exchange followed which was over in seconds. I was very surprised to have addressed this matter so quickly and efficiently. He still had some reservations and slight anger within him, but he seemed to have matured enough to understand what I was saying to him. Funny how it took all of ten seconds to resolve face-to-face that which was impossible over the phone for all this time. After that moment we were inseparable except for times when he needed to go to his own place which was usually late at night. He was then there early every day thereafter. It was so pleasing for me to have this time with my boy. Yeah, even though he's not the perfect son, he's still my boy in the final analysis and I love him with all of my heart and soul!

After that it becomes a big blur of reminiscing, visits and visiting. Whew!! What a whirlwind trip! I needed to fill twenty two years into five days. I almost made it..........do you believe that? I tell you, time went by with lightening speed! Of course it was over before I needed it to be but I remained strong for my family's sake. I refused to cry yet again!

Very soon I was on a plane going back to my precious loves in NY. It had been sometime since I've been away from Raven but never had I been away from Lionel. I couldn't wait to see them. You would think I was gone months! It's amazing how much you bond with your partner. While apart it's always as though something's missing......a part of you. I'm coming home my loves!

THE END

An Immigrant's Tale

Prelude

Many years have since passed and my mother is resting peacefully in a grave in the company of her last born son. My father recently said to me as he looked me squarely in my eyes, "We hope she's in heaven." We were sitting together during a recent vacation trip to Trinidad on the front porch of his house just talking about random things. It was hot and humid with very little breeze yet the air was fresh, refreshingly unlike summer in New York City where the pungent smell of rotted garbage and meats fill your nostrils and mouth as you hurriedly try to make your way to your destination without collapsing into convulsions or vomiting profusely from the stench. I came back at him quickly whilst searching his face for the meaning behind these words, "What? Where else would she be??" My mother was a good woman despite her natural flaws. How dare he say that? He just shrugged his shoulders and said as he averted my questioning glare, "We hope so." I was amazed and said no more on the topic. Who's 'we' anyways? He has changed drastically or maybe I was just beginning to understand who he really is.